THE POLITICS OF PANCHAYATI RAJ ADMINISTRATION

About the Author

Niranjan Pant was the Director, Centre for Development Studies, Lucknow.

He was been doing research in the field of irrigation management since 1975. Initially he was associated with two research institutes, A.N. Sinha, Patna and Giri Institute, Lucknow. In addition, he has worked as a consultant/advisor to National and International organizations such as Ford Foundation, USAID, Planning Commission of India and TAHAL Consultants and the World Bank, Danish, Dutch, SIDA, and NORAD missions.

In the course of research work he has availed visiting fellowships/ research collaboration with Harvard University, U.S.A., SPS and IDE, Japan and WAU, the Netherlands.

The Politics of Panchayati Raj Administration

A Study of
Offiicial-Non-official Relations

NIRANJAN PANT

CONCEPT PUBLISHING COMPANY PVT. LTD.
NEW DELHI-110059

The A.N. Sinha Institute of Social Studies, Patna gave the financial support towards the publication of this work. The Institute however, is not responsible for the views expressed therein.

ISBN: 978-93-5125-270-2

Edition 2026

Published and Printed by

Concept
Since 1974

Concept Publishing Company Pvt. Ltd.
A/15-16, Commercial Block, Mohan Garden,
New Delhi-110059 (India)
T : 91-11-41101460
E : publishing@conceptpub.com, *W*: www.conceptpub.com

FOREWORD

PANCHAYATI RAJ came to be established in parts of India as early as 1959. Subsequently the high hopes put in community development were belied by experience. It was felt that no speedy development, rural or otherwise, was possible unless people were involved in the programme. The panchayati raj was devised as a means for furthering this involvement.

In Bihar panchayati raj was introduced on an experimental basis in two districts in 1965. Even now all the districts in the State have not been covered by the system. There have been a large number of studies, mostly out side Bihar, bringing out the strength and weaknesses of the panchayati raj system. One of the rocks on which panchayati raj seems to have foundered is the relationship between officials and non-officials. Dr Pant in this study has sought to investigate this problem in the field in respect of two blocks in the district of Bhagalpur. He has tried to delineate the sources and areas of conflict and also the areas of co-operation and collaboration between officials and non-officials. He has also tried to find out the reasons for the prevailing state of affairs.

Dr Pant comes to the conclusion that structural reforms are not the panacea for the ills of the panchayati raj. Placing the officials under non-officials, as sometimes suggested, might create problems of greater dimension. What is needed, therefore, is enlightened and committed non-official leadership and efficient and development minded officers. This can only be possible if the larger socio-political culture, of which officials and non-officials are only a part, undergoes significant alteration.

SACHCHIDANANDA
Director

A.N. Sinha Institute of
Social Studies,
PATNA

ACKNOWLEDGEMENTS

THE co-operation of large number of informants, both the official and non-official, was responsible for the completion of this study. I express my thanks to all of them. They were frank and friendly in their responses and many of them went out of their way to help me. Since the information obtained from them was of confidential nature, I am unable to mention their names here.

I express my gratitude to Prof. Sachchidananda, our Director, who provided me with a financial grant and other facilities to make this study possible. I also express my gratitude to Prof. Ali Ashraf with whom I had the benefit of discussing the project at every stage. He also went through the draft report and suggested some valuable improvements.

My thanks are also due to my wife, Lalita, and Dr Mani Bhushan Prasad for their valuable suggestions and encouragement that I received from them.

NIRANJAN PANT

A.N. Sinha Institute of
Social Studies
PATNA

CONTENTS

LIST OF TABLES

ABBREVIATIONS

ADC	:	Assistant Development Commissioner
BDC	:	Block Development Committee
BDO	:	Block Development Officer
BPCC	:	Bihar Pradesh Congress Committee
CD	:	Community Development
CO	:	Circle Officer
DDC	:	Deputy Development Commissioner
DM	:	District Magistrate
MLA	:	Member of Legislative Assembly
MO	:	Medical Officer
MP	:	Member of Parliament
NAC	:	Notified Area Committee
PS	:	Panchayat Samiti
PVP	:	Prakhand Vikas Padadhikari
SDO	:	Sub-Divisional Officer
TA	:	Travelling Allowance
TVS	:	Travelling Veterinary Surgeon
VLW	:	Village Level Worker
ZP	:	Zila Parishad

1

TWO SETS OF FUNCTIONARIES

IN JANUARY 1957, Balwantray Mehta team* was appointed to study and report on Community Projects and National Extension Services from the points of view of economy, efficiency and the extent to which the movement used local leadership. The team submitted its report in November that year. The main conclusions were : (1) sufficient public response was lacking, (2) huge wastage of public expenditure took place; and (3) people did not regard the community development work as their own and consequently did not associate with it.

In order to do away with these shortcomings, the team suggested that the entire rural development work should be placed in the hands of the elected representatives of the people at the village, the block and the district levels. Formation of village panchayats, panchayat samitis, and zila parishads at the respective levels was mooted.

This three tier democratic decentralization scheme sought to transfer all power and responsibility, especially for the execution of development work in the district, to these three bodies at their own levels. Democratic decentralization in essence meant that the power to be devolved on the local body was to be exercised by the popular representatives of the local area.

The Parliament and the National Development Council later discussed this report and accepted its main recommendations.

* Balwantray Mehta, Ex-Deputy Chief Minister of Saurashtra, was a leader of the study team appointed by the Committee on Plan Projects, which itself was constituted by the National Development Council in 1956.

The development work was thus entrusted to the three tier system at the village, block and the district levels, but the States were to adopt it with such modifications as were most suitable to their special conditions. Soon after the term democratic decentralization was rechristened with the more indigenous panchayati raj.

The Panchayat Acts passed by various States were amended in the light of the recommendations made by the Mehta team and the panchayati raj was introduced all over the country after 1957. The Centre issued only general directions about the broad pattern of the system. As a result, there are considerable variations in the timing and structuring of these institutions in different States. Rajasthan was the first State to introduce the system, followed by Andhra Pradesh, Mysore and Tamil Nadu in 1959, Orissa and Assam in 1960, Punjab and Uttar Pradesh in 1961, Maharashtra and Gujarat in 1962, and Bihar in 1964 (in two districts only).[1]

Introduction of panchayati raj brought about a noticeable change in the style, pattern and authority structure of district development administration. During the community development period, preceding panchayati raj, active involvement of the rural people in the development work was desired but the initiative for the plans, policies, programmes and schemes for the local areas came from the officials, and people's role was secondary. Panchayati raj has resulted in the transfer of important powers and functions from the officials to the elected representatives of the people. The officials who used to behave as rulers or 'hakims' earlier are now to carry out the wishes of the people. Now, they have to work along with, often under the direct control of public representatives.

Formerly, officials because of the colonial antecedents manifested paternalistic orientation, haughtiness, impatience and authoritarian tendency in their dealings with the populace. Their interaction with the people was excessively influenced by the consideration of enforcing rules and regulations rather than appreciating and removing the difficulties of the latter. Their style of living, modes

1. In Bihar, the lowest tier (panchayat) of Panchayati Raj has been functioning since 1949.

of thought, and behaviour cut them off from the masses of the people. On the other hand, after century-old dependence on 'hakims', people under the new dispensation have tasted power and freedom and have been made reponsible for performing the duties of administration. As a result of debureaucratization and creation of parallel hierarchies of authority, there is a clear erosion in the prerogatives, powers, and priviledges of the officials.

Historical and socio-cultural factors, however, create an attitudinal gulf between these two sets of functionaries. The lack of literacy, seculiarism, political education and democratic experience only widen this gulf. As early as 1882, Lord Rippon outlining the formation of local self-government, had anticipated a clash of interest, approach and attitude between officials and non-officials.

The pattern of relationship between the officials and non-officials has been an important issue of discussion, debate and investigation. A lot academic and professional attention has been given to it since the sixties. Prominent among the studies on this theme are : B. Maheshwari (1963), T.N. Chaturvedi (1964), M.V. Mathur and Iqbal Narain (1969), Shanti Kothari and Ramashray Roy (1969), V.R. Gaikwad (1969), Iqbal Narain (1970), R.N. Haldipur and V.R.K. Paramahamsa (1970) and K.K. Singh and Ali Ashraf (1971). The scholars agree that the very success of the programme is contingent on the type of relationship between officials and non-officials. The basic postulate of democratic decentralization is that there should be a mutual sense of regard and understanding between the administrative machinery and the respective local bodies. Initiative is to come from the people's representatives and expert advice from the officials.

The actual operation of the programme in various states has presented a picture which is contrary to the expectations and is far from satisfactory. Various reasons have been assigned for this undesirable state of affairs. While most of the scholars view it as malfunctioning of the system, a few consider it a natural process in the transitory stage. They are of the opinion that with panchayati raj, rural society for the first time has been exposed to modern democratic political process. The interaction between the traditional social order and modern political and administrative systems is bound to release new forces and create strains and tensions in the initial stage (Anil Bhatt, 1964).

Those who look at it as the malfunctioning of the system try to find out reasons for the stresses, strains, tensions and conflicts in the organization and structure of panchayati raj bodies and outside it. Different reasons have been assigned by the scholars in this regard. Chaturvedi (1964), for instance, finds cause in the factional politics and officials' involvement in it, and lack of clarity in the demarcation of spheres of action of the two sets of functionaries. While Gaikwad (1969) ascribes socio-psychological factors as the basis of conflict. Roy and Kothari (1969) also find psychological factors responsible for the distrust of one another. An additional factor is the desire of officials to have a say in the policy formulation and the desire of the non-officials to have a share in the implementation of it. Singh and Ashraf (1971) point out that the leaders use resources of local institutions to preserve their own power positions and to further their personal ends. For the fulfilment of these ends, they exercise unfair pressure on government officers. This, according to them, is the main source of tension and conflict in Panchayati Raj. Another reason, they think, is the very diversity of political and bureaucratic cultures that make it difficult for officials and non-officials to work together harmoniously.

Organization of Panchayat Samiti

In Bihar, steps in the direction of introduction of panchayati raj were taken as early as in 1961. The Bihar Panchayat Samitis and Zila Parishads Act, 1961, has under gone modifications from time to time.[2] On account of financial stringency facing the State, the Act was to be implemented in two stages. In the first stage, it was to be implemented in the four divisional headquarter districts of the State, viz., Patna, Muzzafarpur, Bhagalpur and Ranchi. In the second stage, it was proposed to be implemented in the remaining districts of the State.[3] But for reasons best known to the State

2. Major amendments in the Act of 1961 were brought about in 1964 1970 and 1973.
3. Bihar 1963-64, Director of Public Relations, Bihar, p. 92.

government authorities, the Act was implemented only in two districts, viz., Ranchi and Bhagalpur in 1964.[4]

Of all the tiers, the panchayat samiti occupies a crucial position in the entire panchayati raj scheme of Bihar. In conformity with the recommendations of Mehta Committee, the panchayat samiti in Bihar is the principal executive body, relegating the village panchayat to the position of a subordinate agency and the zila parishad to an advisory and co-ordinating agency, providing link between panchayati raj institutions and government.

The panchayat samiti consists of mainly ex-officio members. Accordingly, the mukhiyas of all gram panchayats in the block are its ex-officio members. The other members of the Samiti are : the president of the union board, chairman of the municipality and the vice president of the notified area committee, if any, within the block ; three representatives of the co-operative societies and one representative of the central co-operative bank. In addition, special interests such as scheduled castes and tribes, and women, if such interests or classes are not otherwise represented, and such persons of experience in administration, public life, and rural development, as might be of benefit to the samiti, have to be coopted. Local MP's, MLA's and MLC's have been made associate members without voting right and are not eligible to hold office.

The samiti is constituted for three years. But, a person who becomes a member of the samiti ceases to be one upon his ceasing to hold office by virtue of which he became such a member.

Every panchayat samiti is presided over by a Pramukh (president), who is elected by the members of samiti from amongst themselves. The panchayat samiti also elects an Up-Pramukh (vice-president) from amongst its members. The term of office of Pramukh and

4. In the course of talks with various people, it was found out that Panchayati Raj was adopted only in those districts, which were politically barren. Districts, which had a politically powerful leadership, did not allow introduction of Panchayati Raj. As a result, the idea of introduction of Panchayati Raj in the districts of Patna and Muzzafarpur was dropped.

the Up-Pramukh is three years. However, the State government by an official notification can extend their term.[5] The Up-Pramukh performs the duties of the Pramukh in his absence. In addition to the routine tasks such as convening and presiding over the samiti, the Pramukh is empowered to "exercise administrative control over the Block Development Officer for the purposes of the implementation of the decisions and resolutions of the panchayat samiti and its standing committees".[6] In addition, "the Pramukh shall, at the end of every financial year, send a report as to the work of the Block Development Officer during that year to Collector".[7]

The officials of the samiti belong to three broad cadres: (i) State, (ii) district, and (iii) samiti. The BDO and extension functionaries are appointed by the State government and are in the samiti on deputation. The subordinate technical workers like compounder, vaccinator, health inspector, and ministerial staff are in the separate service cadres of the district. Fourth class employees, like peons are in the panchayat samiti cadre. The BDO is the 'captain' of the team of subject matter specialists drawn from various departments. They are under the operational control of the BDO and the professional control of their respective departments.

The BDO/PVP[8] is the chief executive officer of the panchayat samiti. He is responsible for implementing the resolutions of the panchayat samiti and of its standing committees. He also exercises such powers and performs such other functions as may be entrusted to him by the State government from time to time. The BDO, generally an officer of the rank of deputy or sub-deputy collector and sometimes an agriculture specialist, is under the

5. In Bihar, the elections of Pramukhs and Up-Pramukhs in two districts have not taken place since 1967. Their elections were due in 1970, but have been postponed several times. As a result, Pramukh and Up-Pramukh continue to enjoy an extended term.
6. The Bihar Panchayat Samitis and Zila Parishads Act, 1961, Section 19 (1) (d).
7. *Ibid.*, Section 19 (2) (c).
8. The BDO is drawn from Bihar Civil Service, while the PVP is from Bihar Agriculture Service.

administrative control of the Collector[9] and the Pramukh.

The Samiti functions through eight standing committees[10] constituted each for a group of subjects, viz, (i) agriculture, animal husbandry and co-operation ; (ii) social education, local arts and crafts, small savings and cottage industries ; (iii) public health including sanitation ; (iv) communication and works ; (v) finance and taxations ; (vi) social welfare and programmes for the weaker sections of the people and for women and children ; (vii) irrigation ; and (viii) education. Every committee except those of irrigation and education, consists of not less than five and not more than seven members elected by the samiti from among themselves. The Pramukh is to be a member of the committee on tax and finance, education, and irrigation, and where he is a member, he is ex-officio chairman of the committee. No member, other than Pramukh can be a member of more than two standing committees. The committees are expected to perform such functions as are assigned to them by panchayat samiti.

The functions entrusted to the samiti are municipal, developmental and agency. The panchayat samiti is made responsible for execution and supervision of all programmes under community development and also programmes concerning agriculture, animal husbandry, irrigation, co-operation, education, social education, public health and rural sanitation, cottage industries, inter-village communications, collection of statistics and any other programme for economic and social welfare.

In the Act, various sources of income of panchayat samitis are mentioned. These include grants and aids received from the government, aids received from all India bodies and institutions ; *ad hoc* grants received from zila parishad, grants and funds for schemes and institutions transferred by State government, share of cess and land revenue, donations and contributions received from

9. From June, 1973 to Oct.' 75 in Bihar, B.D.Os worked under DDCs and ADCs in the Panchayati Raj districts. Again, by an ordinance, government restored the power of Collector in Oct.' 75.
10. The Bihar Panchayat Samitis and Zila Parishads Act, 1961, made a provision of six committees. Two committees, viz, irrigation and education were added by an amendment in the Act in 1964.

gram panchayats, municipalities, proceeds from taxes, surcharge and fees leviable by panchayat samiti, income arising from leases granted by the panchayat samiti on public ferries, fairs, *hats* etc. The list, no doubt, makes an interesting reading but the fact of the matter is that grant from the government is the chief source of panchayat samiti income.

It is amply clear from the review of the literature on panchayati raj that unsatisfactory relations between the two arms, officials and non-officials, is a perennial problem. Since panchayati raj is an important feature of the Indian politico-administrative system at the grassroots, the problem needs a thorough investigation to understand the phenomenon and arrive at some workable solutions. Specially in the State of Bihar, such a study is much more necessary, because panchayati raj is still in its infancy here. In Bihar, the Panchayat Samiti and Zila Parishad Act was passed in 1961. The enforcement of the Act has been very low, and it was not until 1964 that this Act was enforced and that too only in the districts of Bhagalpur and Ranchi and later in 1966 it was further extended to Dhanbad district. There was no further progress in this regard until 1973, when it was extended to Palamau, Hazaribagh, Singhbhum, Santhal Parganas and Giridih districts. Twenty three districts are yet to come under the panchayati raj scheme. Coupled with the slow progress in the enforcement of the Act, there is extreme paucity of scholarly concern in the area of panchayati raj. Haridwar Rai and his associates, no doubt, have done some work in this field and one of their research papers (1973) touches upon the relationship aspect in four blocks of Bhagalpur district. But their account is very scanty and superficial.

Two blocks controlled by two different parties have been studied here with regard to the nature of relationship between the officials and the elected members (leaders) at the block level. The major areas of enquiry and analysis were as follows :

(1) To enquire about the sociol-economic background of the officials and non-officials and their attitude and opinions ; (2) To enquire about the sources and areas of conflict between officials

and non-officials. The various sources of conflict may be social, political or legal. As regards various areas of conflict, it may be related to policy implementation, routine administrative matters, utilization of funds and transfer of samiti employees within the block. We also examine the impact of dual and divided authority on the effectiveness of block administration as an agency of development, (3) To enquire about the areas of co-operation and collaboration between officials and non-officials. What are the factors responsible for the co-operation between the two for the public good, and under what circumstances they become active collaborators and utilize their offices for their personal ends? (4) To enquire about the relations between the BDO and his subordinates. If relations are not good between them, there is a possibility of officials aligning themselves with the non-officials and finding support from them. Under such circumstances, it is difficult for the BDO to enforce proper discipline and control. This may have serious implications as regards the effectiveness of the block administration as a unit of integrated development programme, (5) To enquire about the pattern of relation between the Pramukh and other members of the panchayat samiti. We are interested not only in the nature of their relationship but also the basis of the support which the Pramukh gets from other members. The basis of support may be ideological, political, personal or caste-oriented, (6) To enquire about the factors responsible for the dominance of Pramukh or BDO and the consequences of this on the working of the block as a development agency, (7) To make an assessment of the efforts, if any, made for the greater co-operation and elimination of conflicts between officials and non-officials.

In the present research, panchayat samiti (at the block level) has been taken as the unit of study. This choice was guided by several factors such as : (i) the panchayat samiti occupies pivotal position in the scheme of decentralization in Bihar ; (ii) it has been recognized as the basic area unit of the integrated community development programme manned by a team of specialists ; (iii) the block is the area unit of planning and implementation; (iv) it was recommended as the key tier of the panchayati raj scheme by the Mehta Commitee, as far as devolution of power is concerned.

Two panchayat samitis, controlled by Pramukhs of different political parties from one of the panchayati raj districts were selected. These samitis were from two different sub-divisions of the district, one was just a block headquarter, the other was sub-divisional head-quarter. One more dissimilarity between the two panchayat samitis was that one was a shadow package block and the other a non-shadow package block.[11]

This research being a qualitative analysis of the problem rather than quantitative, techniques used in the case study method were applied. Data came from structured short interviews and unstructured depth interviews with officials and non-officials, and others. To supplement interviews, observation technique was utilized. Accordingly, some meetings of the panchayat samiti and of its standing committees were attended with a view to observing the behaviour and actions of the officials and non-officials.

We have also made extensive use of documents. These include records of the proceedings of the panchayat samiti meetings, standing committee meetings, official records and files.

In this study, the term 'officials' covers all the staff working under panchayat samiti. This includes BDO and staff working under him, and Medical Officer and staff working under him. 'Non-officials' include, Pramukh, Up-pramukh, mukhiyas of gram panchayats, and other ex-officio members of panchayat samiti and its standing committees.

To avoid personal reflections, the names used in the report, both for places and persons are fictitious.

11. In Bihar, blocks are categorised into shadow package and non-shadow package. In shadow package blocks, there is greater emphasis on agriculture, and agriculture functionaries are just double in number compared to non-shadow package blocks. Conversion of ordinary blocks into shadow package is done on the consideration of the irrigation facilities in the block and consumption of seeds and fertilizers etc. In the shadow package block, PVP instead of BDO is the captain of the team.

References

Bhatt, A. "Tensions in Panchayati Raj—A comment", *The Economic Weekly*, Vol. XVI Nos. 32 and 33, 1964.

Chaturvedi, T.N. "Tensions in Panchayati Raj : Relation between Officials and Non-officials", *The Economic Weekly*, May 30, 1964.

Gaikwad, V.R. *Panchayati Raj and Bureaucracy : A Study of the Relationship Patterns*, N.I.C.D., Hyderabad, 1969.

Haldipur, R.N. and Paramohansa, V.R.K. *Local Government Institutions in Rural India : Some Aspects*, N.I.C.D., Hyderabad, 1970.

Kothari, Shanti and Roy, Ramashray. *Relations between Politicians and Administrators at the District Level*, I.I.P.A., New Delhi, 1969.

Maheshwari, B. *Studies in Panchayati Raj*, Metropolitan ; Delhi, 1963.

Mathur, M.V. and Narain Iqbal. *Panchayati Raj, Planning and Democracy* ; Asia, Bombay, 1969.

Narain, Iqbal : *Panchayati Raj Administration : Old Control and New Challenges*, I.I.P.A., New Delhi, 1970.

Rai, Haridwar and Prasad, Awadesh. "Panchayati Raj, Bureaucracy and Development : A Study in the Impact of Democratization of Block Administration", *The Indian Journal of Political Science*, July—September, 1973.

Singh, K.K. and Ashraf, Ali. *Bureaucracy, Leadership and Development*, Unpublished report submitted to ICSSR, 1971.

2

SOCIO-ECONOMIC AND ATTITUDINAL SURVEY

OFFICIAL and non-officials bring with them certain values, norms and attitudes which are formed much before they start working together. In the formation of these values, norms and attitudes, socio-economic factors play a very important role.

Social psychologists argue that attitudes reflect predispositions to behave in a particular manner. Attitudes are integrally related to most aspects of social life, carrying expectations about our own behaviour and behaviour of others. Since, attitudes are evaluative predispositions, they condition way people act toward others, programmes they actually undertake, and the manner in which they carry them out. "Thus attitudes are conceptualized as precursors of behaviour, as determinants of how a person actually behaves in his daily affairs[1]". Hence a comparative assessment of socio-economic and attitudinal factors for understanding official-non-official relationships becomes necessary.

Present chapter consists of two parts. In the first part, we compare socio-economic variables of officials and non-officials. It is followed in the second part by an account of their attitudes and opinions about one another and about Panchayati Raj. Here an attempt is made to study the socio-economic variables and attitudes of officials and non-officials, from the point of view of ascertaining their interaction as well as to provide some clues to harmonious and fruitful relations between the two. The observations made here are confined to the two panchayat samitis where we conducted our research. The material presented here is purely of an

1. S J. Cross and M. Niman, Attitude-Behaviour Consistency : Review, *Public Opinion Quarterly*, Fall 1975, p. 358.

illustrative nature. The questions that were asked from officials and non-officials were identical. Therefore, it is possible to make the study of mutual images from the responses of the queries.

SOCIO-ECONOMIC FACTORS

In the present study, socio-economic variables that have been taken for comparison are : age, caste, land holding, income, education, and duration of service in the block. In addition, in the case of non-officials, information was collected regarding their duration as panchayat samiti members and their political affiliations. The data were collected about all the members of the two panchayat samitis (except associate members) and most of the officials working under panchayat samitis, namely, BDO, supervisory staff, clerical staff and field staff (mainly VLWs and Panchyat Sewaks). The break up is as follows :

Members of Panchayat Samitis[2]

	Raja ganj PS	*Veerpur PS*	*Total*
Directly elected members (Mukhiyas)	16	17	33
Ex-officio members	7	4	11
Total			44

Officials

BDO and other supervisory staff	10	11	21
Clerical staff	4	6	10
Field Staff (VLWs and Panchayat Sewaks)	29	30	59
Total			90

2. In the Act there is a provision of co-option of six members. In 1964 when panchayat samitis were constituted for the first time, members were co-opted. But in 1967 and 1971, when panchayat samitis were reconstituted, there was no co-option.

Age

Table-1

OFFICIALS AND NON-OFFICIALS ACCORDING TO AGE

Age Group	*Officials*			*Non-officials*		
	RG	*VP*	*Total*	*RG*	*VP*	*Total*
26—30	8	10	18	—	1	1
31—35	10	8	18	3	2	5
36—40	11	7	18	6	5	11
41—45	9	14	23	1	2	3
46—50	3	4	7	9	5	14
51—55	2	2	4	—	4	4
56—60	—	2	2	2	—	2
61—65	—	—	—	—	1	1
66 and above	—	—	—	2	1	3
	43	47	90	23	21	44

Note : RG, VP and PS respectively stand for Raja ganj and Veerpur panchayat samiti.

The average age of the officials of Raja ganj and Veerpur panchayat samitis is 37.42 and 38.85 years respectively. Similarly, the average age of the non-officials of the two panchayat samitis comes to 45.83 and 45.38 years respectively. Here one thing is noticeable, that there is not much disparity in the average age of officials and non-officials as separate groups in the two panchayat samitis, but there is a marked difference between officials and non-officials on an average. Non-officials are generally from a higher age-group than officials. On an average, non-officials are about 6 years senior to officials. Also to be noted, while maximum number of officials (25.55%) fall in the age group 41-45 years, in case of non-officials maximum (31.81%) come from the age group of 46-50 years. Also, in case of officials, only 14.4% are from the age group of 46 and above, and rest 84.6% are from the age group of 26-45 years. In case of non-officials 54.6% come from the age group 46 and above, while 45.4% come from the age group 26-45 years.

Educational Level[3]

Table-2

OFFICIALS AND NON-OFFICIALS ACCORDING TO EDUCATION

Education	*Officials*			*Non-Officials*		
	RG	*VP*	*Total*	*RG*	*VP*	*Total*
Illiterate	—	—	—	2	—	2
Literate & Primary	2	4	6	2	3	5
Middle & Non-matric	6	6	12	11	13	24
Matric	20	21	41	3	2	5
I. A.	5	5	10	2	1	3
Graduate	4	7	11	1	1	2
Post-Graduate	6	4	10	2	1	3
Total	43	47	90	23	21	44

Taking officials and non-officials as separate categories, we find not much difference in the level of education in the two panchayat samitis. The only noticeable difference is that in Raja ganj panchayat samiti among the non-officials there are two illiterate members, while in Veerpur panchayat samiti there is none. This goes against the general prevalent notion that rural leaders are, by and large, illiterate. On the countrary our case studies show that 86.4% of rural leaders (samiti members) have at least been through middle

3. In the case of technical education number of years the course required are merged with their basic education e.g., medical officer was taken as post-graduate.

school. It is heartening to note that 11.36% of the panchayat samitis members are either graduate or post-graduate.

Nevertheless, when we compare the data between officials and non-officials, we find some noticeable differences. Under-matrics dominate the non-official group (54.54%) while in the case of officials matriculates with 45.56% form the largest group. In case of officials, 23.33% are either graduates or post-graduates compared to 11.36% among non-officials. From the above data, we may perhaps infer, that having a certain level of education facilitates one in occupying leadership positions in the village. This could be thought of as a change from the traditional thinking since one's educational level seems to be getting some recognition for recruitment to leadership positions.

Caste[4]

Table-3

OFFICIALS AND NON-OFFICIALS BY CASTE

Caste	*Officials*			*Non-officials*		
	RG	*VP*	*Total*	*RG*	*VP*	*Total*
Upper Hindu caste	23	23	46	9	12	21
Backward Hindu caste	17	21	38	13	9	22
Scheduled caste	2	1	3	—	—	—
Muslims & Christians	1	2	3	1	—	1
Total	43	47	90	23	21	44

Table 3 shows that maximum number of officials (51.11%) are drawn from upper castes, closely followed by backward castes

4. Upper castes include Brahmin, Rajput, Bhumihar and Kayastha. Backward castes include rest of the Hindu castes except scheduled castes and scheduled tribes.

(42.22%), while scheduled castes and muslims have a negligible number (3.33% each). This is in spite of the fact that in our data majority of the sample consists of petty officials (59 out of 90). The incidence of disproportionately high percentage of upper castes in the rank of high officials is understandable, but even among block level petty officials the high percentage cf high caste officials is very disheartening. Another unfortunate thing is, very low percentage of Muslims and scheduled castes among the officials.

In case of non-officials also, results are not very different from what we find in case of officials. Only difference is backward castes consist of the largest single category (50%) in the sample, but it is closely followed by upper castes (47.73%). Again, as in the case of officials, among non-officials also, Muslims are negligible (2.27%) and scheduled castes are absent. This is in spite of the fact in both the panchayats Muslims and scheduled castes form a significant segment of the total population. In the Raja ganj block there are, 13.83% scheduled castes and 8.69% Muslims, and in the Veerpur block there are, 10.25% scheduled castes, 7.75% Muslims and 3.45% scheduled tribes.[5] On the basis of the above table, we can say that both officials and non-officials are disproportionately drawn from the upper and backward castes and Muslims and scheduled castes are under-represented in both the categories. This, what we find here is similarity among officials and non-officials rather than dissimilarity.

On the one hand, there is lot of talk of the special privileges to the scheduled castes and scheduled tribes in matters of government jobs. On the other hand, sociologists and political scientists have been arguing that as a result of competitive politics the entrenched and dominant castes face a serious challenge from people belonging to lower castes. Unfortunately, the picture that emerges from our data is very frustrating. Scheduled castes, who constitute a significant segment of the total population of both the blocks do not find any representation in the recruitment to leadership positions and are very much under-represented among officials. The greatest beneficiary of the post-independence era seems to be backward castes, who are economically well off and are very well represented among officials as well as among non-officials. Therefore, from the

5. Percentages have been calculated from the 1961 Census.

point of view of social change, backward castes have acquired considerable mobility and scheduled castes, in spite of all the loud talks, have stagnated.

Size of land holding

Table-4

OFFICIALS AND NON-OFFICIALS BY SIZE OF LAND HOLDINGS

Size of land holding	*Officials*			*Non-officials*		
	RG	*VP*	*Total*	*RG*	*VP*	*Total*
No land	14	7	21	1	—	1
Less than 1 Acre	4	4	8	1	—	1
1.0— 2.4 „	10	11	21	2	1	3
2.5— 4.9 „	7	7	14	1	2	3
5.0— 9.9 „	5	14	19	6	3	9
10.0—14.9 „	—	1	1	1	2	3
15.0—24.9 „	1	2	3	5	6	11
25.0—49.9 „	1	1	2	4	5	9
50.0— and above	1	—	1	2	2	4
Total	43	47	90	23	21	44

We find that non-officials have generally larger land holdings than officials. In case of officials 23.33% have no land, while there was only one (2.27%) non-official who did not have any land but he was a rich businessman. Among officials, there are 3.33% who have 25 acres or more land, compared to 29.55% of non-officials who have 25 acres or more land. In case of officials the maximum concentration is in the categories of no land (23.33%) and 1 to 2.4 acre (23.33%), while in case of non-officials, maximum concentration is in the category of 15-24.9 acres (25%), closely followed by 25-49.9 acres category (20.45%).

Another interesting phenomenon that we notice among officials is that in Veerpur panchayat samiti. officials have larger land holdings in comparison to Raja ganj panchayat samiti. For instance, while 32.5% of officials have no land in case of Raja ganj only 14.9% have no land in case of Veerpur panchayat samiti. Also, while 11.6% officials in Raja ganj are in the 5-9.9 acres category, as many as 29.9% officials in Veerpur are in the same category.

Thus, our results show that non-officials have larger land holdings in comparison to officials, and among officials, one panchayat samiti officials have larger land holdings than the other samiti officials. As far as differences in the size of land holdings of officials of two panchayat samitis are concerned, it is difficult to explain these differences. These may perhaps be accidental. But as regards differences in the size of land holdings between officials and non-officials, the main reason seems to be, non-officials are generally agriculturists, hence possess larger land holdings. But this is not true of officials, for them agriculture is a supplementary source of income.

Another notion which is commonly accepted about Indian rural society is that there is coincidence of caste and class. Since land is the most important source of income, let us make a bi-variate analysis of caste and land holdings among officials and non-officials.

Taking officials and non-officials together in our sample, there are 51.4% upper castes, 43.2% backward castes, 2.9% scheduled castes and 2.5% Muslims and Christians. Taking separately, among the officials, there are 53.33% upper castes, 40% backward castes, 4.44% scheduled castes and 2.23% Muslims. Among the non-officials, there are 47.73% upper castes, 50% backward castes, 2.27% Muslims, and there are no scheduled castes and Christians.

Looking at the tables, we find that irrespective of the distinction of officials and non-officials, those who are from the upper castes have larger land holdings in comparison to those who are from backward castes.[6] Nevertheless, the margin of gap is greater

6. In our analysis, we have confined ourselves to upper and backward castes and have ignored scheduled castes. Main reason being, among non-officials there are no scheduled castes and among officials also, their presence (4.44%) is insignificant.

Table-5

OFFICIALS AND NON-OFFICIALS BY THE SIZE OF LAND HOLDINGS AND CASTE

	Landless		*Less than 1 acre*		*1-2.4 acre*		*2.5-4.9 acre*		*5-14.9 acre*		*15-49.9 acre*		*50+acre*		*Total*
	Offi-cial	*Non-off.*	*Offi-cial*	*Non-off.*	*Offi-cial*	*Non-off.*	*Offi-cial*	*Non-off.*	*Offi-cial*	*Non-off.*	*Offi-cial*	*Non-off.*	*Offi-cial*	*Non-off.*	
Upper caste	4	—	7	—	9	1	10	2	14	5	3	11	1	2	69
Backward	14	1	1	1	9	2	4	1	6	6	2	9	—	2	58
Scheduled caste	1	—	—	—	3	—	—	—	—	—	—	—	—	—	4
Muslims/Christians	2	—	—	—	—	—	—	—	—	1	—	—	—	—	3
Total	21	1	8	1	21	3	14	3	20	12	5	20	1	4	134

among upper and backward caste officials in comparison to their counterpart non-officials. Among the officials, we find 29.17% of upper castes in the category of 5-14.9 acres land, while only 16.67% backward castes find a place in this category. This difference is much more conspicuous when we take account of those who have no land. Among the upper castes, 8.33% fall in this category, while 38.89% are drawn from backward castes in this category. Among the upper castes, the largest concentration (29.17%) is in the category of 5-14.9 acres of land, while among backward castes, the largest concentration is in the category of landless (39.4%). As regard scheduled caste officials, none have land exceeding 2.4 acre. Difference exist in case of non-officials also, though, these are not as marked as in case of officials. Among the non-officials, 52.38% upper castes are in the category of 15-49.9 acre, while 40.91% backward castes fall in this category.

Income[7]

Table-6

OFFICIALS AND NON-OFFICIALS BY TOTAL INCOME

Income	*Officials*			*Non-officials*		
	RG	*VP*	*Total*	*RG*	*VP*	*Total*
Upto Rs. 300	8	3	11	1	1	2
301—500	23	23	46	9	4	13
501—700	5	12	17	2	1	3
701—900	4	2	6	1	1	2
901—1500	1	6	7	4	9	13
1501—2500	1	—	1	3	3	6
2501—3500	1	1	2	2	1	3
Above 3500	—	—	—	1	1	2
Total	43	47	90	23	21	44

7. In case of officials, income from sources other than salary is also included.

Looking at table 6, we find that non-officials are richer than officials. Also, officials and non-officials of Veerpur have generally more income than their counter-parts in Raja ganj. This disparity in the income level of officials of the two panchayat samitis is understandable when we take into account the fact that Veerpur officials have generally larger land holdings. Since they have more land so they can supplement their income more than Raja ganj officials. But the disparity in the income of the non-officials of the two panchayat samitis is inexplicable. In case of Raja ganj officials, average monthly income is Rs. 525.81, while that of Veerpur officials's average monthly income is Rs. 582 09. Similarly, in case of Raja ganj non-officials, average monthly income is Rs. 1230.44, while that of Veerpur non-officials is Rs. 1338.10. The most noticeable feature which the table presents is, non-officials are far richer than officials. Average monthly income of officials is Rs. 555.20, while that of non-officials is Rs. 1281.82, which is more than double. This is an interesting finding in the light of low income of rural masses in India. This means that rural leadership is drawn from the richest sections of our village society.

In addition to the above queries, information about the political affiliation and term of office of the panchayat samiti members, and duration of stay in the block, and home place in case of officials was also obtained.

All the non-officials are residents of the block since birth except one each from both the panchayat samitis. But both of them are residing in the block for the past twenty years. In case of officials, because of the transferable nature of their job, the duration varies from less than one month to more than 23 years. Generally the supervisory and clerical staff have a smaller duration than field staff. Panchayat sewaks have generally the longest duration. The average duration of officials in case of Raja ganj panchayat samiti is 3.98 years, while in case of Veerpur panchayat samiti, it is 5.50 years.

A major portion of clerical and field staff comes from the same district (72.46%) and considerable portion comes from the same block (26.09%). While majority of the supervisory staff (79.19%)

come from outside district and only 19.05% come from the same district. This is in conformity with the government rule, according to which, VLWs and panchayat sewaks are generally appointed and transferred within the district. Another government rule is that no staff should be posted in the 'thana' where his own home falls. But there are some exceptions to it, mainly because of *pairvi**, which is a very common phenomenon in Bihar.

As regards political identification, most of the panchayat samiti members claim to be members of Congress (R), 14 out of 23 in one, and 17 out of 21 in the other panchayat samiti. This is inspite of the fact that the Pramukh in the Raja ganj panchayat samiti is from Congress (O), but he is the lonesome Congress (O) member. This means that support or opposition in panchayat samiti is not on party lines, but on personal, caste, and factional lines. The position of other party members and independents is presented in table 7.

Table-7

NON-OFFICIALS PARTYWISE

Political Party	*Raja ganj PS*	*Veerpur PS*
Congress (R)	14	17
Congress (O)	1	1
Independents	4	3
Jan Sangh	1	—
C.P.M.	1	—
C.P.I.	2	—
Total	23	23

* *Pairvi* is the process of influencing a decision in one's favour with or without the help of an intermediary. Formerly it was resorted to only in special circumstances but now it is a common phenomenon and sometimes leads to miscarriage of justice.

In table 7, it is clear that no other party occupies any significant place in any of the two panchayat samitis.

The elections for panchayat samitis were held three times since their creation in Bihar, i.e., 1964, in 1967 and 1971. In our sample, there were certain members of samitis, who were Mukhiyas before 1964 and thereby members of BDC, because Gram Panchayat Act was operative in Bihar since 1949. But for our purposes, we have taken 1964 as the starting point, because it was from 1964 that three tier structure was started in Bihar in two districts. So, the total terms of panchayat samitis for our purposes are three. The term-wise position of panchayat samiti members is presented in table 8.

Table-8

NON-OFFICIALS TERMWISE

Panchayat Samiti	*Terms*			*Total*
	One term	*Two terms*	*Three terms*	
Raja ganj	10	8	5	23
Veerpur	12	4	5	21
Total	22	12	10	44

One significant point that emerges from table 8 is that, in case of Veerpur panchayat samiti majority of the members (12 out of 21) have only one term, while in Raja ganj panchayat samiti majority of the members (13 out of 23) have either two or three terms. The logical conclusion, on the basis of these facts, would be that there is greater circulation of elite in Veerpur. But fact of the matter is different. There has been enormous increase in the number of Rajput members in Veerpur samiti in the elections of 1967 and 1971. The reasons of the increase have been discussed in greater detail in Chapter 4.

ATTITUDES AND OPINIONS

Under the panchayati raj programme, officials have not only to work for the people but they have to work with them. People's representatives under this scheme share equal responsibility of rural development alongwith officials. Since the task of rural development is shared by these two sets, their mutual images and opinions about one another will affect their working relationship considerably. It is essential that the approach and outlook of both officials and non-officials towards one another are properly oriented to get maximum and quick results. If both are willing to understand and appreciate each other's difficulties, there is bound to be a healthy relationship proned to greater accomplishments.

Before we start analysing their views, it would be appropriate to mention certain important points about the sample and mode of analysis. It was not possible for us to interview all the persons for whom socio-economic and other data were collected and which we have analysed in the first part of this chapter. In case of officials, out of 90 we interviewed 53 (58.89%) and in case of non-officials, out of 44 we interviewed 25 (56.82%). Thus, in both the cases, almost similar percentage of officials and non-officials were interviewed. Another point which is pertinent from the point of view of mode of analysis is that, in case of socio-economic data, we have tabulated it separately for the two panchayat samitis, but in case of present analysis, we have merged it together. It was done mainly because of two reasons. Firstly, the total number of interviews was much less so it was not possible to break it further to smaller categories. Secondly, and which was main consideration for doing so, we did not find any significant difference in the attitudes and opinions in the two panchayat samitis.

Analysis of Responses of Officials and Non-officials

Table 9 : Do you think, you are fully supported by officials and panchayat samiti members in things you wanted to do in public interest, or you have to face many obstacles and difficulties ?

In case of officials we asked them about panchayat samiti members and when interviewing panchayat samiti members we asked them about officials. Thus, this single question will explain about each other's mutual images.

Table-9

Respondents	*Full Support*	*Indifference*	*Obstacles*	*Total*
Officials	35	10	8	53
Non-officials	17	5	3	25
Total	52	15	11	78

The majority of the officials and non-officials feel that they are fully supported by their counterparts. 66.04% officials and 68.00% (almost similar) non-officials feel that they are fully supported by their counterparts. 18.87% officials and 20% non-officials feel that they are shown indifference and 15.09% officials and 12% non-officials feel that obstacles are created in their way. It is significant to note that one third of the officials as well as non-officials are not satisfied with the role played by their counterparts.

Table 10 : Do you think that block officers and employees generally take sufficient personal interest in the development works pertaining to the area ?

Table-10

Respondents	*Yes*	*No*	*Total*
Officials	40	13	53
Non-officials	14	11	25
Total	54	24	78

The above table indicates that while three fourth (75.47%) officials speak favourably about themselves, 44% non-officials speak negatively about them.

Table 11 : Do you think that Panchayat Samiti members generally take sufficient personal interest in the development work pertaining to the area ?

Table-11

Respondents	*Yes*	*No*	*Total*
Officials	23	30	53
Non-officials	19	6	25
Total	42	36	78

From the above table we can interpret that three fourth (76%) of non-officials speak favourably about them, while less than half (43.4%) officials speak favourably about the non-officials. Now, when we compare the results of this table with that of the previous one, we find quite similar findings. In both the cases, three fourth officials and non-officials speak favourably about them. Only difference we notice is when they speak of their counterparts. Here we find, non-officials assess their counterparts little more favourably than officials assess non-officials. While 56% of non-officials speak favourably of officials, 40.40% officials speak favourably of non-officials. It may be because of two reasons. Either the officials are not favourably disposed towards non-officials, or non-officials really do not take as much interest as they should.

Table 12 : Do you think that panchayat samiti members help officials in mobilising financial and human resources for development programmes and to make them acceptable to the people ?

Table-12

Respondents	*Yes*	*No*	*Total*
Officials	28	25	53
Non-officials	19	6	
Total	47	31	78

The officials would, no doubt, be put at ease if they get help from the panchayati raj leaders in the mobilization of both human and financial resources not only for implementation of development programmes but also for these programmes being accepted by people at large. Our analysis of the responses shows that more than half of the officials (52.83%) think that panchayati raj leaders are helpful in this regard. At the same time 76% of the leaders themselves think they are helpful.

Table 13 : Generally speaking, do the officials extend support to one another or they are given to mutual rivalries and jealousies ?

Table-13

Respondents	*Support*	*Rivalry and Jealousy*	*Total*
Officials	48	5	53
Non-officials	19	6	25
Total	67	11	78

For the efficient working of block administration not only there should be cordial relations between officials and non-officials but also among officials themselves, there should be co-operation and support rather than rivalries and jealousies. Our query reveals that 90.57% officials feel they support each other. Three fourth of panchayat samiti members also feel that officials support each other. We can infer, generally speaking officials support one another, which is very encouraging for the morale and efficient working of the bureaucracy.

Table 14 : Do you think that people often put pressure on officials for improper demands ?

Table 14, reveals that 26.41% officials and 12% non-officials were of the opinion that people exert pressure for improper demands. Those who mentioned people use pressure, invariably cited instances where people pressed for more agricultural loans in spite of the fact that they had not repayed the previous loans.

This, we do not think can be regarded as pressure for improper demands, more than that, it is a manifestation of their helplessness.

Table-14

Respondents	*Yes*	*No*	*Total*
Officials	14	39	53
Non-officials	3	22	25
Total	17	61	78

Table 15 : Do you think that panchayat samiti members often put pressure on officials for improper demands ?

Table-15

Respondents	*Yes*	*No*	*Total*
Officials	24	29	53
Non-officials	5	20	25
Total	29	49	78

If we compare the responses of this table with that of preceding it, we find that a greater number of officials as well as non-officials feel that panchayat samiti members exert pressure on officials for improper demands. Here, nearly half of the officials (41.51%) and one fifth (20%) non-officials express the view that panchayat samiti members exert pressure on officials. Also, here unlike people, pressure is really for various kinds of improper demands, generally leading to gratification of self, friends or kins.

Table 16 : Do you feel that the services of competent and efficient officials are recognized and rewarded ?

The degree of commitment and sincere devotion to work would definitely depend on the sense of satisfaction enjoyed by the officials and on the reward system. On the basis of table 16, if we compare the responses of the officials and non-officials

Table-16

Respondents	*Yes*	*No*	*Total*
Official	22	31	53
Non-officials	23	2	25
Total	45	33	78

we find great disparity. As against 41.51% officials, 90.00% non-officials feel that official's services are recognized and rewarded. Main reason of this dissimilarity in the thinking may be because, non-officials feel that if some official does good work he receives public praise ("wah, wahi"), so it is a recognition and reward for his service. On the other hand officials think it from the professional career point of view i.e. promotion etc., in the service.

Table 17 : Do you think that panchayati raj should continue, or it should be abolished, or it does not make any difference whether it is abolished or it continues ?

Table-17

Respondents	*Continue*	*Abolish*	*No difference*	*Total*
Official	23	20	10	53
Non-official	21	2	2	25
Total	44	22	12	78

The success of the panchayati raj in general, and good relation between officials and non-official in particular, depends considerably upon how they perceive the programme and what they think about its continuance. We find, marked differences in the response of officials and non-officials in this regard. Among those who think it should continue are, 43.40% officials and

84% non-officials. While 37.73% officials think it should be abolished, only 8% non-officials (they also because they think panchayat samitis have neither finances nor powers) advocate its abolition. Similarly, 18.87% officials think it does not make any difference as against 8% non-officials who think so. Quite expectedly, we find a much larger percentage of non-officials, who think panchayati raj should continue than officials.

To summarise, we find non-compatibility between officials and non-officials not only with regard to socio-economic traits, but also, we find marked differences in their attitudes and opinions, which sometimes are diametrically opposed. As regards socio-economic traits, officials are generally more educated and younger in age, while non-officials are generally less educated, older in age but richer, compared to officials. In the attituditional sphere also, both officials and non-officials think negatively about each other. Officials in general are not ready to accept the people's representatives on equal terms. Their attitude towards the elected representatives is that of contempt and resentment and consider them as a hurdle in their efficient working. On their part, non-officials also resent the superior air of officials, and their refusal to accept non-officials as their superiors.

3

RAJA GANJ : THE PRAMUKH—BDO SYNDROME

OFFICIALS and non-officials cannot be treated as two dichotomized groups. In every situation, and more particularly of conflict, there are groupings which are generally interpenetrating and cross cutting the official, non-official demarcation. At the same time, they maintain their separate identity as exclusive categories of officials and non-officials, covertly opposed and antagonistic to the powers and privileges of the other group.

One significant point that emerged from our study is that Pramukh and BDO who head these two teams at the panchayat samiti level are the two chief actors of panchayat samiti politics. Their good or bad relations symbolise good or bad relations between officials and non-officials at the panchayat samiti level.

BDO and Pramukh

At Raja ganj the Pramukh has been holding office since 1967 and the present BDO since January 1972.[1] By and large, relations between the two have been cordial. There have been occasional tiffs and on two occasions serious differences between the two. The relations between the present Pramukh and the BDO, who preceded the present one and who also stayed in the block for more than three years, were reported to be still better. Since the present BDO spent almost four years in the block, we would confine our study to this period only.

Most of the officials and non-officials who were interviewed in

1. The BDO's transfer coincided with the completion of our study in that block.

detail, were of the opinion that the relations between the two were generally good. It is generally believed that the Pramukh and the BDO, both are accommodating type. They try to adjust with each other and generally do not come in each other's way. One member of the panchayat samiti said, "Both help each other. For instance, in giving schemes and other block facilities, the BDO has always favoured the supporters of Pramukh. Similarly, the Pramukh has never bothered about, why the BDO uses the block jeep for his private trips to the district headquarter ?" Another said, "They have good relations because the Pramukh gets work of his group people done by the BDO and on his part the Pramukh helps the BDO by appreciating the work of the BDO when big officers come for inspection. On such occasions, the Pramukh as public representative, presents a very rosy picture of the block."

Most of the officials as well as non-officials feel that the Pramukh is not corrupt, because he is very rich. Nevertheless, they feel, he might not take in cash but he enjoys such facilities with the BDO as merry making trips to the district headquarter for booze and movies and parties by rich businessmen of the area with whom the BDO is very friendly.

About the Pramukh, the general feeling is that he least bothers about public work in the block. The Gram Panchayat Supervisor mentioned that during the last nine years as Pramukh he has never visited any Gram Panchayat. In the Panchayat Samiti meeting, which was attended by the author, the Pramukh was asked by the leader of the backward castes to inspect schools and make his findings known to the members of panchayat samiti.

As regards dominance, the general feeling is that the BDO dominates over the Pramukh. The BDO is said to be a shrewd man, who keeps the Pramukh in his grip. He knows more rules and regulations than the Pramukh does. In addition he is in the good books of his superiors and even if the Pramukh reports against him, he sets things right at higher official levels. The Pramukh does not have a clear cut majority to support him in the panchayat samiti. Whatever support he has is on the caste and personal grounds. A lonesome member of the Congress (O) his main political asset was an uncle of his, who was at one time President of the BPCC. The leader of the backward castes in the panchayat samiti, and who holds an important office in the district Congress Committee, is always on his toes to oust the Pramukh. So, the Pramukh has to depend on the BDO for the support. The BDO is in an advantageous position because he "keeps some mukhiyas in his pocket." He is in a position to oblige these mukhiyas by giving them contracts of minor development schemes where he has a free hand. In addition, the BDO has no enemies in public, has friendly relations with the rich businessmen of the area, and good reputation as a sincere and devoted worker among his superior officers.

The BDO appears to be the most powerful man in the block. He looks on public representatives with contempt, as uneducated boors and thinks, "BDO has the power to get the Pramukh arrested with hand-cuffs." Opinion about him is that he is a man who believes in show off and knows how to take work from others. But he himself has not much devotion to the public work and is more concerned with his personal gains. It is felt, till civil supply work was under BDO, he liked his job as BDO. Once it was taken away from BDO and given to the Circle Officer[2] (CO), he was disinterested in his job and started trying for his transfer and eventually got him transferred as Circle Officer in another block.

An important thing about the BDO is that though he has been more concerned with his personal ends he has also done well in the sphere of public work and has earned a good reputation among the residents of the Raja ganj. Not only, he knew how to take work from his subordinate staff but he also knows how to utilize non-official. He mentioned, "In the development work the Pramukh extended fullest possible support to me. Some times when I have found myself handicapped, I have used his (Pramukh's) services, e.g., he can write to the higher authorities anything and there is no restriction for him. I made him write

2. Circle Officer is in the charge of revenue collection work at the anchal level, and the area of anchal is coterminus with block.

to ministers and other higher authorities, criticising the concerned officers that they were sleeping and were not doing anything. In Zila Parishad also he has considerable influence because the Adhyaksha and the Pramukh owe allegiance to the same party. So, I have utilized this advantage of his official position in the furtherance of development works in the block."

On occasions of differences between them, in majority of the cases the BDO has scored over the Pramukh. On some occasions he has done so with the help of superior officers. For instance, in case of transfer of a touring veterinary surgeon in spite of 'tooth and nail' opposition from the Pramukh the BDO got him transferred. On other occasions he has manoeuvred the support of majority of the members of panchayat samiti and has outwitted the Pramukh. For instance, in the case of T.A. payment to the driver of the block jeep. The Pramukh did not want the money be paid to him on the ground that the duty involved 'law and order', so the Pramukh thought it should be paid by the SDO office and not by the panchayat samiti. But the panchayat samiti passed a resolution for the payment.

The BDO is reported to be a shrewd and resourceful man, who gets things done, mostly the way he likes, either with or without the support of the Pramukh. For cordial relations between the two Pramukh needs him more than he needs the Pramukh. As mentioned earlier the main reason of the Pramukh's greater dependence on the BDO is that the Pramukh does not have a clear cut majority in the panchayat samiti. Under such circumstances, a clever and tactful BDO is bound to be in an advantageous position. To quote the words of a member of the panchayat samiti, "If every action of Pramukh is backed by the panchayat samiti then Pramukh scores over BDO, and if it does not happen BDO can manoeuvre things in his favour." This applies very truly in case of Raja ganj panchayat samiti.

Though, good working relations exist between the Pramukh and the BDO but both grudge each other in their private talks. The BDO thinks, the Pramukh unnecessarily interferes in his administrative jurisdiction. On his part the Pramukh feels the BDO does not take him into confidence to the extent he should.

BDO and other Officials

Relations between the BDO and his subordinates are said to be purely of superior-subordinate type. They obey him out of fear and not out of respect. Even the veterinary doctor who gets more salary and is older to him addresses him, "Sir", and hesitates before entering his room. The BDO's relations with his supervisory staff are impersonal and business-like. He rarely takes them out with him and is never found mixing with them in a friendly manner. All staff fear him so much that no body dare go against him though most of the staff is not very happy with him. The supervisory staff, in particular, does not like his authoritarian attitude. They claim that they are also of officer cadre and he is simply a co-ordinator of the team and therefore, should co-operate with them rather than boss over. They recall the previous BDO who not only co operated with them but also went out regularly on field visits with them. The Pramukh felt, "As far as supervisory staff is concerned, they dread him. They cannot do anything except murmuring against him."

One of the main grievances against the BDO is that he uses jeep mostly for his personal work but when asked by the supervisory staff for genuine official work they would be reproached so much that they would never ask again. One supervisor explained his difficulty, "In our departmental meetings we are told to ask for the jeep for better performance of our job, and our department pays some annual money for the consumption of petrol for this purpose. They do not believe us when we tell them that we are not given the jeep and ask for the proof. So, once I asked the BDO about the jeep in writing. He called me in his room and reprimanded me so much before every body, as if I had committed a great offence."

An important aspect of relations among officials is the feeling of specialists vs. generalists. This generates a sense of greater intra-service solidarity among the subject-matter specialists and generalists. Since, district administration is headed by a generalist (DM or DDC), specialists feel that they are relegated to the background and are harassed by the generalists. One subject-matter specialist lamented that, "He (BDO) always threatens us that he would report about us to the DDC, get us suspended or, make bad entry in our confidential report. We can't do anything against him. Because, even our district officers have to work under DDC and since both DDC and BDO are civil service people so DDC gives more importance to BDO."

Comparing the present BDO with the former one, the Pramukh said, "He (previous BDO) was honest. He did not misuse the jeep and when went out for field visits, used to take concerned supervisor with him. His attitude towards the staff was that of co-operation and not authority. But he (present BDO) tries to keep them in his grip by threats, so they work only half heartedly." The leader of the backward castes said, "He has such a tight grip over them (staff) that no body can speak anything against him."

The BDO's relations with the present medical officer incharge are good. The MO is quite young and is very sincere about his work. He is a friendly type without any ego problems and gives due respect to the BDO. But the BDO's relations with previous two MOs were said to be far from cordial. Main reason was that they did not like the BDO's bossing around and did not accept him as their officer. They thought as medical and health incharge, their staff was fully under them, while the BDO thought, as the leader of the official team at the block level he was overall incharge.

The BDO is accepted by all his subordinate staff as their real immediate boss. This may be because of the fact that no body could ever score a victory over the BDO. With or even without the Pramukh's support he has given "lessons" to the defiant staff. In case of a MO with whom he had no good terms and who had opened a private dispensary in the market place, the BDO got him close it with the support of the Pramukh. Though, in this case majority of the panchayat samiti members were helping the MO. In another case, he got a Travelling Veterinary Surgeon transferred, despite the fact the Pramukh went out of the way to oppose this move of the BDO. This he did with the help of his superiors.

It is pointed out that though office clerks are status-wise below supervisory staff but they are treated better. On their part the office staff feel that the BDO does not take into confidence all of them equally. It is pointed out that the BDO's favourite in the office is a clerk who deals with scheme files. This man is said to take share from each contractor, who is given any construction scheme through the agency of the block. The head clerk resents that he is never taken into confidence by the BDO in these matters. This clerk, it is pointed out, has been a favourite of the BDO since very beginning. Till supply of essential commodities was under the block,[3] this clerk was also dealing with supply matters. This clerk is here for the last four years, and now his transfer has coincided with that of the BDO.

About the BDO, it is felt that he is very resourceful and knows how to keep his superiors happy. It is pointed out that after civil supply was taken away from the block and given to the Circle Officer he made lot of "pairvi" with the collector, and with his help got him transferred to another block as CO. Main reason that was pointed out by most of the interviewees was that he did not find BDO's job as paying as that of CO's.

As regards the BDO's relations with the field staff (mainly VLW's and Panchayat Sewaks) ; it appears, he does not have direct relations with them. Their fortnightly meetings are presided over by their respective supervisors, viz., Agriculture Officer and Gram Panchayat Supervisor. Of the lot who come to attend their meetings in the block head quarter, hardly any one is required to meet him.

Generally the BDO is not liked by his staff and more particularly by his supervisory staff. They complain he talks in a friendly manner with people who serve his interest. One supervisor pointed out, "The supply clerk who is a lower division assistant of the Circle Office talks so freely with the BDO. No other person can do so." There is no question of bad relations with the BDO because no one can afford it. On the surface, relations

3. Civil supply was taken away from the BDO and was placed under the CO in January 1975 in Raja ganj block.

between the BDO and other officials seem to be alright but there is great dissatisfaction with the manner the BDO behaves with them. Apparently there is only one clerk who is close to him. One staff commented, "No body's words have greater weight than Hari babu's. If he tells you that your work would be done, then your work will be done, whether you are a staff member or an outsider."

Panchayat Samiti Politics and Administration

At present there are 25 members in the panchayat samiti. Of these 16 are directly elected mukhiyas from as many panchayats in the jurisdiction of the samiti. Seven are ex-officio members[4] and two are associate members, one MP and one MLA in whose constituency the panchayat samiti falls. But these two members neither attend the meetings of panchayat samiti nor have voting rights, so, for all practical purposes panchayat samiti consists of twenty three members who have voting rights and who attend panchayat samiti meetings.

Scheduled Castes who are 13.83% of the population are not represented at all in the samiti. Whereas with just one member the 8.69% Muslims are grossly under represented.

The Pramukh, one of the richest men of that area was elected to the post in 1967. Then Congress was undivided and he was the nephew of an ex-BPCC (Bihar Pradesh Congress Committee) President who was also chairman of the erstwhile district board. He is from upper caste, and though upper castes are not in majority in the panchayat samiti but he managed to win the election by one vote. Following Congress split in 1969 the Pramukh remained the sole member of Congress (O) but he remained unaffected and continued to remain in power. Thanks to the support by some upper caste mukhiyas, and one muslim mukhiya who have always stood by him. At the panchayat samiti level, support or opposition is not on party lines. It is mainly on personal and caste considerations.

4. Of the ex-officio members, three are from co-operative societies, one from Central Co-operative Bank, one from Vyapar Mandal and other two are, Vice-chairman of notified area committee and Pramukh.

All members of the panchayat samiti can be divided in three groups. There are those who support him irrespective of the merit of the case, these are as already mentioned, upper castes and a muslim member. Then, there are those who are opposed to the Pramukh and would like his down fall. This group consists mainly of backward castes and is led by the man who was defeated by the margin of one vote in the election of Pramukh in 1967. He resides in the NAC area and has been ex-officio member of the samiti for the last ten years in different capacities. The third group consists of neutrals or "opportunists", as they are called by some members. This consists of intelligent and clever people who side with the Pramukh, the BDO or the backward caste group, depending on the circumstances. This group does not have any leader and is not an organized one.

The Pramukh is not a very educated man but he has good understanding of the Act and rules and regulations governing panchayat samiti. He has no superior air about him and behaves well with every one who approaches him. Politically he knows his limitations, so generally does not cross his limits. But once he decides about something he remains stubborn about it and fights it out regardless of the result.

The two most active members of the panchayat samiti are, vice-chairman of the NAC (ex-officio member) and the leader of backward caste group in the samiti. The NAC vice-chairman is graduate and is a teacher in the local college. He is very suave and polished man, and knows what to say, where to say, and how to say. He has considerable influence in the meetings of the panchayat samiti. He is a vaishya and should be in the backward group caste-wise, but he is said to be a supporter of Pramukh. It is said, the Pramukh helped him in his election and he helps him in return. But he has not supported the Pramukh on each and every case. He is in the good books of both, the BDO and the Pramukh.

The leader of the backward caste group, though only middle school pass, is very articulate and has very good idea of the statutory provisions and rules and regulations concerning panchayat samiti. In the samiti meetings, he puts his arguments intelligently and forcefully. He is a soft spoken, has no pretensions. Economically he is quite well off (engaged in ghee business and has a vegetable farm in the block) and politically resourceful. He is an office holder in the District congress (R) committee and has links with some important Congress (R) leaders at the State level.

The Up-Pramukh, is a simpleton. He is from a backward caste and his election was a unanimous choice, because he has always been neutral. Generally he supports the Pramukh and does not do anything which is "injurious to the prestige of panchayat samiti". He does not appear to have any influence in the samiti politics. In the absence of the Pramukh, when he presides over the samiti meetings he is relegated to the background. His political consciousness appears to be very low. His horizon is very limited and does not see beyond his own village. Following dialogue which the author had with him will further illustrate the point.

Up-Pramukh	:	"Today a minister is coming".
Author	:	"Yes, Chief Minister Jagannath Mishra is coming".
Up	:	"What is the name of the Chief Minister" ?
Author	:	Dr Jagannath Mishra".
Up	:	"Is he a doctor also"?
Author	:	"No he is not a medical doctor. He has doctorate in economics".
Up	:	"I see".
Author	:	"Don't you know the name of the Chief Minister"?
Up	:	"Yes, I know. His name is also in the currency notes (he meant S. Jagannathan Governor of Reserve Bank)".
Author	:	"No, he is not that man. He is a different man altogether".

(This incident took place when Dr Jagannath Mishra was already in office for about 6 months).

The panchayat samiti meets after every two months as a matter of routine. To facilitate district level officers to attend the meetings, the annual roster for the meetings of each panchayat samiti is prepared by the DDC in the beginning of the year for the whole district. Among the non-officials, most of the mukhiyas and other ex-officio members attend the meetings but not the associate members. During the past two years for which records were examined, the MP did not attend any meeting and the MLA only once (that too becuase there was a special invitee in the meeting that day). Among the rest, there were two regular absentees and two remained absent in every third meeting. Rest were regulars. On an average, 15 to 17 out of 23 non-official members were present in the meetings. Maximum number was nineteen and minimum was eight.

The author attended two meetings of the panchayat samiti. In the meetings, only four or five members were active and rest were silent spectators. First meeting was presided over by the Pramukh and the Agriculture Officer was deputed by the BDO on his behalf because he was out of the block. Second meeting was presided over by the Up-Pramukh and the BDO was present in this meeting. In the first meeting there was no outside officer, either from the sub-divison or from the district, but in the second one, there were three or four officers from outside. In both the meetings few members were active. The BDO was the most conspicuous figure of the second meeting. He could turn a discussion to any direction or close it if he so liked. In fact he had boasted, before the meeting. "I don't permit them (members) to go out of the way. I have told them if any member would use impolite language I would turn him out. You would see how I handle them. I will conduct the whole business within fifteen minutes. I will finish off every thing *chutki bajate* (within no time)".

The Up-Pramukh, no doubt, presided over the second meeting but his role was simply ritualistic and he did not make any comment throughout the meeting. The NAC vice-chairman and the leader of the backward caste group were the chief spokesmen of the samiti on both the occasions. They initiated the matters, provided the samiti with facts and worded its resolution. At the outset of both the meetings resolutions of the previous meetings were read and confirmed. It was followed by the secretary (BDO) reading out official letters concerning the panchayat samiti, concerned officers from outside (from district and sub-division) acquainted the members about the new schemes and programmes they were undertaking and sought members' co-operation.

The BDO is not just the secretary of panchayat samiti but he is also its guide. He guides members on technical matters, permits questions which could be discussed in the panchayat samiti and also gives sense of direction to its discussions. On many matters he puts his foot down and does not permit samiti to discuss. A clever BDO will always frustrate members' designs if he does not feel these proper. Sometimes the BDO is absent from meetings and resolution are passed in his absence and noted down in the proceeding register. In case he does not like, he puts his own comments on the margin. Two of such resolutions passed by the panchayat samiti in a meeting in which the BDO was absent and which were not acceptable to him are as under :

(1) "Samiti considered the matter concerning the progress of the work of Mr Sitaram (VLW). It unamiously supported his work and it was decided to recommend his satisfactory progress to higher authorities." The BDO put his own note on the margin : "It is an administrative matter and the samiti should not discuss it. The samiti can discuss only matters concerning development works."

(2) "Mr Mohan and Mr Sohan, two mukhiyas gave a joint resolution to the samiti that recent transfers of VLWs be cancelled immediately to make present rabi campaign a success. In future in matters of transfer the advice of the concerned mukhiya be taken before decision regarding transfer is taken. It was passed Unanimously." In this case also the BDO had put a similar note as in the above case.

According to the BDO, such resolutions are passed because concerned officials make direct approach to the mukhiyas and mukhiyas take their case without realizing the fact that such things encourage indiscipline among the officials. "If my staff start feeling that I cannot punish them, why will they obey me"? In such cases, where the BDO feels that the samiti has gone beyond its legitimate powers he puts his dissenting note, otherwise compliance of the resolutions is noted on the margin.

One of the general complaints in the samiti meetings is that the concerned officers from the district and sub-division do not attend the meetings. One of such resolutions reads :

> "Industries extension supervisor is regularly asked for attending meetings. Information in this regard is sent to the district industries officer and the DDC but no action has been taken in this regard so far. Therefore, it is unamiously decided that he should be given a reminder, and information about it be sent to higher officers."

Generally resolutions passed by the panchayat samiti are confirmed in the next meeting. However, sometimes, samiti rescinds its own resolutions. In one case it did so, both on technical and moral grounds. The matter involved the inclusion of a person as farmers's representative in the Block Agriculture Advisory Committee. In the previous meeting, someone who was a convicted by the High Court in a murder case, was co-opted in this committee. In the next meeting the leader of the backward caste group objected to this co-option on both legal and moral grounds. A special meeting called within a fortnight unanimously decided to seek the advice of the government lawyer in this regard. In the next meeting the BDO informed that the matter was sent to the DDC because the government lawyer would not give his advice to the panchayat samiti directly. In the meeting, when a member asked the BDO his opinion about the matter. He replied, "When he is not eligible to be a member, how can he be co-opted."

Resolutions are passed by the samiti either unanimously or by majority vote. There are instances of resolutions passed with Pramukh's note of dissent. In one instance the matter referred to the payment of T.A. of the driver of the block jeep. The BDO wanted to make the payment but the Pramukh did not agree. The Backward caste group leader brought the matter in the samiti and asked why the payment was not made (the bill was pending for a year). The Pramukh informed, the duty performed by the driver concerned law and order and was done on the order of the SDO, so payment should be made by the SDO's office and not from the samiti fund. Since the BDO and SDO had passed it, samiti also permitted the payment. Pramukh's note of dissent ran thus : "This resolution for the payment is wrong. I am opposed to this payment. Hence, this resolution may be sent to the DDC and only after his direction payment should be made." In the next meeting the BDO informed the samiti that the DDC had permitted the payment so the bill would be cleared immediately. This according to the BDO was a well deserved a humiliation for the Pramukh, only because of his obstinacy.

Investigation in matters of public interest also sometimes figure the panchayat samiti resolutions. Here, it plays an important role as a custodian of public money. Raja ganj block is situated by the side of the Ganges, so during rainy season when the river swells, the whole area gets flooded and crop gets damaged. There is a very old *kachcha* dam to protect the area from the ravages of flood. It has been repaired many times and every year some money is spent on it. In a samiti meeting, one member asked whether it was correct that in year 1975, Rs. 65,000 was spent on the repair (just filling the gaps with soil so that water may not leak out from these points). The BDO informed that according to the Executive Engineer Rs. 1,65,000 was sanctioned for that purpose but they spent only Rs. 1,05,000 and saved Rs.60,000. This information agitated members very much, as virtually no work was done and whatever little patch work was done would not have required more than 10,000 rupees. They felt that they were saved not because of the repaires but because of the fact that the Ganges water did not rise more. The NAC vice-chairman dictated a reso'ution : "After seeing the work, the panchayat samiti has reached the conclusion that Rs. 1,05,000 which is spent on the work does not justify it. In 1972 and 1973, Rs.20,000 and Rs. 26,000 respectively were spent and much better work was done. Therefore, the samiti unanimously decides that an enquiry be made concerning the money that was spent. A copy of the resolution be sent to the Collector, the DDC, the Concerned Officer, the Chief Minister and the anti-corruption committee."

The BDO did not agree to the idea of sending a copy to the anti-corruption samiti. It was pointed out by the CO that it would create a bad precedence, and if legally it was not possible then it would be a stigma to the secretary (BDO). The BDO said, resolution should be respectable as well as useful and dictated another resolution : "An enquiry be made regarding the expenditure incurred in the repair of the dam, and it be repaired in such a way so that it could be used both for protection as well as for irrigation purposes."

Thus, we find that panchayat samiti could be used as a forum, both for furthering vested interests as well as being guardian of public interest. If properly utilized and members are conscientious about their duties and obligations, samiti could play an effective and useful role.

To facilitate the working of the panchayat samiti, there is a statutory provision for eight standing committees. The most important of these are committees on finance and tax, irrigation, and education. All the influential members find place in these committees.

One of the general complaints in the samiti meetings has been that the members lack enthusiasm to attend committees meetings. It is pointed out that the members generally do not attend these meetings. In one of the samiti meetings the Pramukh was authorised to reconstitute these committees and replace such members who did not attend the meetings. In another meeting six months after it, the BDO informed that dates were fixed for the meetings of all the eight committees in that month but none met because of the lack of quorum. The BDO's attributed absenteeism to the fact that membership of these committees was imposed on them and they did not like it, so they did not attend. The decisions these committees take are quite important as far as block level officials are concerned. For instance, the education committee recommends transfers of the school teachers. The finance committee sanctions T.A. bill and other types of arrears and bills. Matters like increase in the dearness allowance of the samiti employees, are also sanctioned by the standing committee on finance and tax. It also prepares the annual budget of the samiti.

The meetings of the samiti and its standing committees are called by the BDO on the instructions of the Pramukh. However, on one occasion, the Pramukh asked the BDO for a meeting but the BDO refused. This situation arose because the DDC had asked the BDO to send all the papers concerning a matter. The Pramukh wanted to discuss this matter in the Finance and Tax Committee, whether the file should be sent to the DDC or not and wanted the BDO to withhold the papers till then. The BDO refused to call such a meeting on the ground that according to the Bihar Panchayat Samitis and Zila Parishads Act 1961, Article 64, the Collector in whose place the DDC is appointed, is empowered to demand any record or report from the BDO. Again, according to the Bihar Government letter No. 4340 dated 8.5'73, this point has been repeated. Here the ADC is also empowered to demand any such paper. Therefore, it was outside the jurisdiction of the samiti to review the powers and obligations of the ADC. On the BDOs refusal, the Pramukh called a meeting with his own signature. But when the meeting took place the Pramukh did not attend this meeting.[5] Since the Pramukh himself was absent so, after discussion, the members left the matter as it was and no decision was taken.

An important dimenson of panchayat samiti is the induction of politics in administration. Many times, panchayat samiti has been used by individuals for furthering their personal interests. Panchayat samiti is a small body so officials develop informalities with the members and use them individually or as a body. In one case, the block overseer had got him transferred by *pairivi*. The BDO and the Pramukh were not ready to relieve him till a substitute was provided in his place. In one of the panchayat samiti meetings in which both, the BDO and the Pramukh were absent, the overseer managed the following resolution passed in the panchayat samiti.

"The samiti discussed the transfer of Mr Ram Singh, Overseer of the block. The samiti unanimously passed the resolution that Mr Ram Singh's wife has been ill continuously and since he has been transferred to Darbhanga six months back, samiti recom-

5. The Pramukh told later, in an interview, that he did not pursue the matter any further because he had reconciled with the BDO in the meantime.

mends he be relieved, and requests the DDC to order his charge be taken over by the zila parishad overseer immediately". Though the BDO's note in this regard was that it was an administrative matter and the samiti could not discuss it and the samiti could discuss only matters concerning development work. But when the matter reached the DDC he accepted the decision of the panchayat samiti.

On another occasion the BDO humbled the Pramukh with the support of the influential members of panchayat samiti. The matter referred to the payment of block staff's salary. Fresh grant had not come and 'Holi' festival was near. The BDO wanted to make the payment by the diversion of funds of other items. This was not acceptable to the Pramukh and technically he was right. The BDO consulted the members of the Finance Committee and some "important members of the samiti." They agreed and the BDO made the payment despite the Pramukh's objection.

These were the cases in which members's use as a body (samiti) was made. But many times the Pramukh's 'pairvi' or links with the Pramukh are utilized by the officials. The MO pointed out, "There is one man in my staff from whom I cannot take work properly because I know he is the Pramukh's man". This fellow is a *jat bhai* (caste fellow) of the Pramukh and has been working in the block for a long time without being transferred. In another case, the Pramukh went to the ZP President for the 'pairvi' of a clerk to get him transferred near his home. He succeeded in his mission mainly because the ZP President and the Pramukh are members of same political party.

Sometimes forces outside the panchayat samiti also play important role in the panchayat samiti politics. On one occasion, serious differences had developed between the Pramukh and the BDO on account of cancellation of an auction decision arrived at by the BDO. In this case the BDO was humiliated, and as a matter of fact, this was one of the few instances in which the Pramukh prevailed upon the BDO. The BDO in this case had to redo the whole thing (auction of mango grove). After this case, the BDO coaxed the members of samiti that they should start a signature campaign for the Pramukh's ouster and he would be with them. In this case the BDO had succeeded in getting even some upper caste mukhiyas to sign against the Pramukh. On this occasions, the CO came to help the Pramukh (CO was not pulling on well with the BDO). The CO has influence over those members of samiti who are grain dealers and also those who are not because he is incharge of the supply of essential commodities at the block level. Most of the mukhiyas have their 'give and take' relations with dealers so even those mukhiyas who are not dealers are under the influence of CO. Therefore, the CO's help came handy to the Pramukh and the BDO's design could not succeed.

Thus, we find the panchayat samiti as a forum is used, both for public and private interests. At times the Pramukh and the members of samiti are used by officials for their personal advantages. Though the BDO may criticise that the staff make use of non-officials for their personal works but he himself is not lagging behind any body in using members for his personal interests, and his unique position in the set-up gives him an extraordinary advantage in this respect.

4

VEERPUR : ONE VERSUS MANY

IN THE preceding chapter, we discussed the case of Raja ganj panchayat samiti. In the present one, we have taken up Veerpur panchayat samiti and have discussed it in similar fashion. Like the preceding chapter, the present one is divided into three parts. Part one covers the relations between Pramukh and BDO/PVP. Part two deals with BDO/PVP vis-a-vis their staff. In Part three, we have discussed the panchayat samiti politics and its impact on the administration. In case of the present panchayat samiti, the description is slightly different in comparison to Raja ganj panchayat samiti. There, we confined our discussion to one BDO. But in case of the present samiti, we have talked about four—two BDOs and two PVPs, who were incumbents of the office in the samiti in different periods of time. This, we had to do for two reasons. Firstly, the present PVP's duration here is of few months. Secondly, those who preceded him during the past five years, were very important for understanding the totality of official, non-official relations.

Pramukh and BDO/PVP

The present Block Pramukh has been in office since 1967. But, we would be taking into consideration only those BDOs/PVPs who worked with him during the past five years, viz, 1971 onwards. During this period, two BDOs and two PVPs worked with him. Throughout our discussion, we would refer them as the first BDO and the second BDO. Similarly for the two PVPs also as the first and the second.

The first BDO came to the panchayat samiti in 1968 and remained there till 1972, i.e., for almost four years. The Pramukh was a mukhiya from 1964 and unsuccessfully contested the Pramukh's election that year. He tried again in 1967 and won. In 1969, when mid-term assembly elections took place, he got the Congress ticket for the local constituency and won. The releations between the BDO and the Pramukh were reported to be very friendly. "There was hardly a day when they did not meet. As soon as the Pramukh's jeep entered the block office, the BDO and his wife would run out to receive him", told an old staff.

During the period when this BDO stayed in the block, the Pramukh is reported to have made lots of money by doing all kinds of irregular work. Many schemes were received during this period like, relief, block quarters repairs, irrigation etc. One ex-member of the samiti said, "Out of twenty eight irrigation wells for the whole block twenty were located in the Pramukh's gram panchayat. But these remained only on paper. All the money was eaten away by the Pramukh." Schemes which were for the benefit of the poor farmers are said to have been given to a particular contractor (Mota Babu). Under one of such schemes, 20 to 25 wells were sanctioned to the block. In case of these wells, 75% of the total cost was given by the government and remaining 25% was to be spent by the individual farmers. These schemes were started for the benefit of the poor farmers. The BDO and the Pramukh, it is alleged, gave the construction work of all these wells to Mota Babu, who formed the trio with them. It is pointed out by most of the interviewees that during 1971, lots of money was sanctioned to the block for the relief work but most of it was not spent for public work. Schemes existed only on paper, or work was done only for namesake. The kachcha roads were made and payment was made for the pitched roads. One member of the samiti said, "In the period of the first BDO eighteen scheme of the value of Rs. 9,999 were given to Mota Babu because if any scheme exceeded Rs. 10,000, it could not be executed by the panchayat samiti". Another said, "Two hundred and forty schemes of the first BDO's period are still pending in our block and for these advance payment was already made". Most of the persons felt that the Pramukh did all sorts of bungling during this period because most of the schemes of the block were given to the family members of the Pramukh or to the contractor, Mota Babu.

About the BDO, there was a feeling that he himself did not make money. He was from a rich and respectable family. His father was a district magistrate and mother was a member of the assembly during the British period. He merely obliged the Pramukh. The schemes are reported to have been given by him on the instructions of the Pramukh. At that time the Pramukh had an overwhelming majority in the Panchayat samiti. In addition, he was also the MLA. Most of the people felt that the BDO wanted Pramukh's 'political backing' for his promotion. Another reason which was mentioned by an old staff was, "BDO's wife had considerable influence over him. She was a butterfly who regularly came to the BDO's office chamber, and interfered in his work. Even in cases, where he was reluctant to do the job, she would insist him to do. Mota Babu had put a car at the BDO's disposal and he used to go out frequently with his wife for pleasure trips."

The second BDO, who joined after the transfer of the present one, stayed in the block for a short period of six months. His relations with the Pramukh were very bad. When he joined, he could not get possession of BDO's official quarter because the previous BDO's family was still living there. By caste he was a *Chamar*, and the Pramukh was a *Rajput*, so, he felt that it was deliberately done to humiliate him. Besides, this BDO was a very strong willed man and would not succumb to any kind of pressure. Once, the Pramukh asked him to give two bags of sugar to a dealer. The BDO declined to do so without checking the records, and did not give sugar to that dealer because he found many irregularities in his records. The BDO refused to oblige the Pramukh in shady deals.

Their rift was further widened when this BDO sent papers concerning all the irregularities and bogus schemes, which took place during the previous BDO's time, to the higher authorities. It was on account of this that anti-corruption department started enquiries regarding these irregularities. According to a staff, who worked during that time, "He was a hard working officer and would not give the Pramukh a free hand to make all kinds of loot. He was a Deputy Collector and was very much conscious of his administrative powers." When he was transferred, the Pramukh wanted him to give the charge to the CO with whom the Pramukh was friendly. The BDO stubbornly refused, and for one day charge was given to some magistrate in the sub-division ; who, next day handed it over to the CO. The Pramukh had tried for his transfer, no doubt, but the main reason for his transfer was the conversion of the block to a 'shadow package' block, and a man from agriculture side was required there, designated as PVP.

The new man, who came to the block was a PVP. He joined in the first quarter of 1973 and remained there till march 1975. Relations between the Pramukh and the PVP still worsened. During his two years stay, he worked with such a zeal and dedication for the welfare of the people that he became an instituion in that area. Among the officials, the non-officials and the public at large he was esteemed so much that they felt there could never be another PVP like him in the whole Bihar. He worked with a missionary zeal and was honest to the core. One ex-member of the samiti said, "He was so honest that he would not accept even a cigarette from any body. He worked so much with the people because he worked in the field and not just sat in the chair." He used to tour extensively but rarely using the jeep. A staff of his time said, "Pradhan saheb, during his whole stay, did not use the jeep for more than twenty times. Before him about 30 thousand rupees annually must have been spent on the jeep. He used to tour on foot, by rickshaw or by bus. If he had used the jeep all the time, many times staff would have been deprived of their salaries." During his stay, whatever work he took he completed it before he left. One informant said, "He took eighty irrigation wells during his time and got all of these completed except nine, for which he had not made any advance payment. And all these are working very well even now. This is a history in itself. It was mainly because he inspected and made close scrutiny of these works when these were in progress and would not make any payment unless he was satisfied. In spite of all sort of pressures he was never detered in his spirit. If all officers were like him heaven will come down to earth."

Such a man would not be party to any misuse of power. Naturally his relations with the Pramukh worsened. The BDO would not himself do anything irregular, nor would he permit any body do so. The first such instance was when the Pramukh wanted his personal jeep to be repaired and the payment for it to be made from the panchayat samiti fund as the repair of the block jeep. The BDO did not agree. Secondly, when inquiries started taking place with regard to the previous irregularities the Pramukh wanted him to conceal the facts. But he did not do so and did not give any file to the Pramukh to destroy the facts. The climax of deterioration of their relations reached, when a majority of the samiti members passed a vote of no confidence resolution against the Pramukh. After the resolution, the Pramukh is alleged to have entered in the PVP's room with one of his lieutenant members, abused the PVP and forcibly took away the register in which this resolution was noted. The SDO, the thana incharge and all the police force who were there, were silent spectators.

The Pramukh had started making efforts for PVP's transfer just after a few months of his joining. He was transferred twice, but the public representations to the higher authorities in Patna went in favour of his staying in the block, and on both the occasions his transfer was cancelled. On the second occasion, it was reported, the leader of the anti-Pramukh faction personally brought the cancellation letter from Patna. Despite the better relations between the two, which had reached a peak with no confidence motion incident, the PVP continued to remain there for another one and a half year, and left only when he found, it was impossible for him to make full utilization of his efforts for the multifarious development of the block.

His successor, the present PVP joined a few months back and so far there has been no rift between him and the Pramukh. He is said to be a hard working but accommodating type. Presently there seem to be cordial relations between the two. The Pramukh co-operated with him recently when he wrote a letter to the Chief Engineer, Bihar, regarding the repair of the block office roof from which water was leaking out and official papers were unsafe. The PVP had written several letters in this regard but nothing was done. But the Chief Engineer took immediate action after the Pramukh wrote a demi-official letter to him. The Pramukh also wrote an appreciation letter to the agriculture minister praising the PVP's work in the sphere of agriculture.

Many reasons are mentioned for the existence of cordial relations between the two. The present PVP is a Brahmin having relations among the State's high ranking politicians and officials. While the previous two incumbents were lower in the caste hirarchy. The first one was a Chamar and the second was a Yadav. In addition, they did not have resource networks at higher political and administrative levels like the present PVP. Secondly, very short time has passed to test the validity of their cordial relations, and no such thing has occurred which might bring their self interests into conflict. Also, the Pramukh rarely comes to the block, particularly after the no confidence motion incident. Further, the PVP has been more than attentive to the demands of the Pramukh's supporters in the panchayat samiti. The most forceful reason appears to be the one expressed by an old supervisory staff. He said, "The Pramukh had so much of troubles with the previous two BDOs that he can not afford to spoil his image any more. He is an MLA and the election might take place any moment. Also, his financial difficulties have passed. Now he possesses a car and a jeep with other avenues open for making money."[1] On his part PVP gives him every respect that he can give and does not mind doing little favours to the Pramukh's lieutenants.

As regards dominance, in the period of the first BDO it was the Pramukh who was all in all. But the two incumbents who followed him did not succumb to the Pramukh's pressures. In the case of the present PVP, though there has not been any interference but the PVP appears to be quite sensitive to the "wishes" and "recommendations" of the Pramukh. Since, it is pointed out that the Pramukh does not interfere, so there is no question of dominance. But the Pramukh's short visit to the block office, to which the author was a lucky witness, was sufficient to prove that the PVP was a dwarf before the towering figure of the Pramukh, and his 'presence' even in his physical absence was a living reality.

1. Many interviewees mentioned that the MLAs work as brokers. They charge a fix amount for getting things done in the government.

BDO/PVP and Staff

During the first BDO's period relations between the BDO and his staff were generally satisfactory. There were one or two exceptions but otherwise there was no problem. His relations with the Head Clerk were the best. There was perfect tunning between the two. Since many irregular works were done during that period so it was natural that the Head Clerk and the Scheme Clerk were nearer to the BDO. Even those few who were dissatisfied did not show their resentment against the BDO because of the fact that the BDO and the Pramukh had a close affinity.

Since the second BDO and the Pramukh could not pull on well and most of the staff was loyal to the Pramukh, the BDO found it difficult to get co-operation from office staff, particularly from the head clerk. He wanted to prepare records of all the irregularities of the previous period so that papers could be sent to the higher authorities. For this purpose, he needed people who were loyal to him and on whom he could depend. Therefore, he used to bring records and files to his residence, and used to work during the night with the help of supervisory and field staff. His relations with most of the supervisory and field staff were reported to be good though he was strict to them because of his authority-consciousness.

When the first PVP joined, he found similar difficulty with the office staff. They would leak out the official decisions and would try to conceal facts. The office staff was pro-Pramukh so they used to reveal office secrets. Official letters were not put before him in time. Therefore, he requested the DDC that unless most of the office staff were transferred, it would be difficult for him to do any work. Gradually most of the office staff, and such other staff, who did not co-operate with him were transferred.

His relations with his staff were ideal. He co-operated with them in every possible way. All those officials who worked with him recall that he did not have any superior air about him. There were only two exceptions in the whole staff with whom he had some problem. One was a cashier, who neglected his work so much that the PVP was forced to relieve him of his duties. The other was the veterinary surgeon who was a favourite of the Pramukh and used to indulge in politics all the time and rarely attended his office. He is reported to be the Pramukh's chief advisor and confidant in the Pramukh's quarrels with the PVP. He was transferred in 1974 and was relieved by the PVP in his absence on the ground he was absconding. The department asked the PVP to send all the necessary papers so that disciplinary action could be taken against him. But the Pramukh with all his resources not only managed to let him remain in the block but also, the PVP was forced to pay him the salary of the period for which he was treated absent from the duty.[2] Barring the veterinary surgeon the whole staff co-operated with him and were whole-heartedly with him in his conflicts with the Pramukh, though not manifestly but in a covert fasion.

As regards the present PVP his overt relations are good with his staff. He gives due respect to every body, particularly to the supervisory staff. He does not behave like a boss to any one of them. His relations with most of the staff are that of a team leader, who is willing to co-operate with any of them in the discharge of their duties. He chats with and treats his supervisory staff like colleagues. There is no one in the staff who fears him. He is hard working, takes his seat in the office right at 10 a.m., when most of the staff is yet to arrive. He disposes papers very promptly and generally does not keep any papers pending. For his field visits, he is equated with the PVP who preceded him. Unlike the BDO of Raja ganj panchayat samiti, he presides over the meetings of the panchayat sewaks and the VLWs. These meetings last for two to three hours and he himself discusses all schemes and programmes with meticulous details with them. Nevertheless, when it comes to comparing him with the other three BDOs who preceded him, he does not rank very high. The three most important reasons which are mentioned for his comparative low ranking are, he favours certain staff, he is corrupt, and he does not trust his office.

2. The DDC's note to the PVP in this regard was that the Veterinary Surgeon "was holding office in the block on the orders of the Pramukh. Therefore, the payment for the period due, be made at the earliest and he (DDC) be informed about it."

He is said to depend wholly on a Block Agriculture Officer. This man was ranking low in the eyes of the previous PVP, who had once caught him in the bungling of fertilizers. This Agriculture Officer is said to be the present PVP's class-mate, and is a close friend and confidant. "Any scheme or work or any decision, even if it was a minor one, would be taken only after consultation with Arun babu (Agriculture Officer)", commented a staff. This undue importance to Arun babu is resented by all the staff mainly because the PVP is so much in the grip of Arun babu that if they want anything, it could not be obtained without Arun babu's green signal. A staff said, "He (PVP) does not have any administrative capacity, he just goes on talking. If, I don't do any work he should take action against me but he does not have that capacity. Once, the area people had complained against the concerned VLW that he did not visit the field. He called the clerk and dictated a note asking the VLW's explanation. Meantime, Arun babu came and told that when he went to the field he found VLW there. Hearing this from Arun babu, he took the note and tore it off. The reason was, that VLW was a *chela chapati* (disciple) of Arun babu."

It is reported that the PVP makes money through Arun babu. Arun babu is reportedly telling every one from whom he takes money that 50% share of the money goes to the PVP. Comparing him with the first BDO, a VLW said, "He used to help the Pramukh in making money and that too in big schemes but this fellow is so mean that he does not spare even the small schemes. It seems he will sell out the block." A technical staff confirmed this, "In the past, I gave him a share from what I got from the contractors."

His office staff resents his lack of trust in them. Once, the author was sitting in the office when a clerk showed a file to the Head Clerk telling him that a particular letter from it was taken out by the PVP. Both resented this. The head clerk suggested him to note down that the letter was taken out by the PVP. The clerk who was custodian of that file, thought it improper on the part of PVP to take out that letter without telling him.

On his part the PVP appeared to be satisfied with most of his staff. But he felt, "There are some staff who know how to befool the BDO as well as the non-officials. They consider themselves intelligent because such people befool both the sides. They indulge in politics and are successful in getting away with it, they get their travelling allowance regularly. Such people are most dangerous. Activities, of such people must be closely scrutinized. Not only they harm the BDO but public work also suffers because of them. That is why I am trying to test such people". The PVP's relations appeared to be quite good with every one in the staff. Only exception was the veterinary doctor, with whom he hardly had any relations. He is in the block for almost six years and his transfer is over due.[3] He is still reported to be not attending his duties in the office. Some supervisory staff complained about this thing to the PVP, who on his part complained to the Pramukh but it did not make any difference in his work style.

The PVP's sreputation as an efficient and hard working officer, is very high. He is first in the district in many programmes and activities. He has many letters of appreciation commending his job. The Pramukh of the samiti where he worked before his present assignment, on his transfer, wrote a letter to the Zila Parishad president that he should not be relieved at that juncture, because the block work would suffer. In this samiti also he has received letters of appreciation for his agriculture work.

As far as BDO and MO relations[4] are concerned, there has not been much scope for conflict, mainly because there has never been an MO incharge at the block level except for short intervals. Most of the time during the last five years, the family planning doctor has been looking after the block medical and health work also. But he is not under the administrative control of the panchayat samiti. As a result, there is very little formal link between him and BDO, and they seldom meet.

3. There is a State Government circular that a government servant posted at a particular place should not continue to remain there for a period more than three years, normally.
4. This includes PVP also. When we talk of particular persons, we have used the designations BDO or PVP as the case may be. Otherwise BDO includes PVP also.

One dimension which is important here is the relations between the office staff and the field staff. Like the previous panchayat samiti the relations appeared to be not smooth. Once the author was sitting in the office, when a VLW came to a clerk's table with a villager for his work. The clerk told him to come again. Hearing this the VLW burst out, "I have come here today, only for his work, otherwise I would have come here tomorrow. Why do you harrass us so much, *kitni bhookh hei thumhari* and how will it be satisfied ? You don't consider VLWs anything. We promise the people and bring them here and here you people are so gready."

Panchayat Samiti Politics and Administration

At present, the panchayat samiti consists of twenty two members. Of these seventeen are directly elected members, one Pramukh, who is also a sitting MLA from the area, three representatives of the co-operatives and one associate member, who is the MP of the area. The MP has not attended any meeting of the panchayat samiti during the past two years for which we collected the record. There is no representative of the municipality and the central co-operative bank. In the former case, the elections have yet to take place and in the latter case, no fresh elections have taken place.

We find no muslim and no scheduled caste and scheduled tribe representation in the samiti. This is, despite the fact that there are 10.26% scheduled castes, 3.45% scheduled tribes and 7.75% muslims in the population of the block (calculated on the basis of 1961 Census). Thus, 21.46% of the population is unrepresented in the present samiti. On the other hand, Rajputs, who constitute roughly 15% of the population[5], have 50% of the directly elected posts. If we study the caste pattern in the three panchayat samitis, which have been constituted since its inception in 1964, we find progressive increase in the number of Rajput mukhiyas. Table 18 indicates the number of mukhiyas on the caste basis.

5. Based on the information given by the Gram Panchayat Supervisor.

TABLE-18

MUKHIYAS CASTEWISE IN THE THREE PANCHAYAT SAMITIS

Castes	*1964-67*	*1967-71*	*1971-till present*
Koeri	5	4	1
Jaiswal	3	1	—
Yadav	2	2	4
Rajput	2	5	8
Kurmi	1	1	1
Kayastha	1	—	—
Muslim	1	2	—
Teli	1	1	—
Brahmin	1	1	2
Kalwar	—	—	1
Total	17	17	17

The above table clearly shows how Rajput mukhiyas have progressively increased from two to eight. This abnormal disproportionate increase in their number is reported to be the result of unfair elections. The present Pramukh being a Zamindar of the area allegedly used force in the elections. The leader of the present rival faction was then the chief commander of his 'operation force'. They would either capture opposite party's booths or would not allow the opposition candidate's voters to caste their votes. Most of the places, where backward castes were in majority and the Rajputs were an insignificant minority, Rajputs won through foul play and unfair elections. In this game of foul play, the officials openly helped the Rajputs, mainly because the then BDO was a henchman of the Pramukh. The officials helped the Rajputs in several ways e.g., giving them unused ballot papers, unfair counting, etc. The first Pramukh (1964-67) mentioned that in his own election, the leader of the present rival faction, who was then the chief commander of the Pramukh's *lathiat* force (force equiped with sticks), captured one of his booths and gave it to the opposite party.

As regards the quality of non-official members of the panchayat samiti ; most of them are dull and inarticulate. One member, for instance, did not know about the existence of the two Congress parties. He took the two factions in the samiti as two Congress parties. Three members were cases of chronic sickness, and one was too old to attend to his duties so most of his work was done by his son. Only one third of the members were active, and were equally divided in two factions. Rest of the members were either 'hand raisers' (blind supporters) or chameleons that changed their colours as it suited the situation. The spineless hand raisers on the other hand never dared to go against the Pramukh or the *babu bhayyas* (young Rajputs) who are opposed to the Pramukh.

During the past one year and ten months for which the records were available ; on an average, 15 of the 21 non-officials attended the meetings of the samiti. The officials's participation in these meetings on the other hand was very poor. Only when the DDC or the ADC attended the meetings, did some district level officers participate in the samiti meetings, otherwise rarely did they attend. Bulk of the officials who participated in the meetings where either from the block or the sub-division. During this period nine ordinary meetings of the samiti took place. On an average, 6.1 officials out of 29 (who were expected to attend) attended the meetings. The range varies from maximum attendence eight, and minimum attendence one. It was a common complaint that the officials did not attend panchayat samiti meetings. A typical sample of the non-officials's grievance is reproduced below :

> "The district, the sub-division and the block level officials who are the members of this samiti do not take interest in its meetings and do not consider it necessary to take part in its meetings. As a result, members remain ignorant about the departmental activities and schemes. In this regard, authorities's attention has been drawn earlier. After preparing the roster of the meetings, it has already been sent to the official members. Under such conditions, their absence is regreted by this samiti, and once more competent authorities are requested to give due

attention to the absence of these people."

Generally, resolutions of the panchayat samiti refer to routine administrative matters concerning the block staff and its schemes and programmes, and are mostly passed unanimously. But sometimes factionalism gets too much reflected in the samiti resolutions. For instance, in one of the meetings, two members of the Pramukh faction raised an objection against the secretary (the first PVP) delaying the notice instead of issuing it before the mandatory ten days. One of the members even charged that the notice was back-dated. The resolution said that the charge appeared to be true.

In the next meeting, it was noted in the register that the minutes of the previous meeting were read and confirmed. But below it was a note which said that when the question of confirmation of the items came, the leader of the opposition group objected to the confirmation of that particular item. The Pramukh without any voting adjourned the meeting. The note further said that nine out of sixteen members who were eligible to vote opposed it, and requested the matter be taken up in the next meeting of the samiti.

The next meeting, which was presided over by the Up-Pramukh passed the resolution : "The resolution of the meeting of 15-10-74 was not confirmed though mention of its confirmation is made in the register on 28-12-74. Therefore, this meeting decides that from the passed resolutions of 15-10-74, item 1 (A)[6] is rejected. The resolution No. 2 of 28-12-74 in which mention of its confirmation is made is also rejected. The meeting confirms the proceedings of 28-12-74 with above amendments in the proceedings of 15-10-74". This resolution was passed by a majority vote.

The matter did not end here, and in the next meeting again objection was raised by the two pro-Pramukh. It was permitted by the president that the opinion of the higher officers would be sought in the matter for the constitutional clarification. This case clearly shows that the pro-Pramukh faction wanted to humiliate the

6. This referred to the charge made against the PVP that he back-dated the notice for the samiti's meeting.

PVP, while the anti-Pramukh faction wanted to show their full support to him so that no stigma is attached to the PVP.

To understand the factionalism at present, it would be better to go back to past and trace its origin. When 1971 elections of the panchayats took place, there were only five contestants who were opposed to the Pramukh. Of these, two lost and only three got elected. The Pramukh used to say openly in the panchayat samiti meetings that out of 17 mukhiyas 14 were his own men and three were opponents. These three were, Hari Singh, the Up-Pramukh and Dal Badlu Singh, all Rajputs. That was the time when the Pramukh was all powerful. He was already an MLA and had a 'yes man' as the BDO. Then he used to do whatever he liked. One ex-member of the Finance Committee said, "He used to get our signatures in the register and later used to fill in whatever he liked. Once I said, I will put my signatures only after decisions are noted down. After that he used to decide, either without calling me or without calling any meeting." That time he had an overwhelming majority support, which was not wholly on caste lines, though Rajput mukhiyas had increased considerably after 1971 election.

Another and more important reason was that he had become an MLA in 1969 and his political influence had increased considerably and the BDO toed on his line. It was during that time, he neglected his opponent mukhiyas completely. One such mukhiya who was opposed to the Pramukh told that he was harassed and humiliated in several ways by the Pramukh and the then BDO. He was the only mukhiya whose oath ceremoney was not attended by the BDO. All work for his panchayat, he told, was done through the ex-mukhiya, who was a favourite of the Pramukh. For instance, the relief money was distributed by the BDO among the panchayat people with the help of the ex-mukhiya. Whenever, the BDO or the Pramukh visited his panchayat, they went to the ex-mukhiyas's house. He was not even invited in the farewell party of the first BDO, which was "grander than a marriage ceremony."

Factionalism in the Pramukh's group arose mainly because of the rift that developed between the Pramukh and his chief lieutenant

Neta Singh. Neta was an unknown figure before 1967 and was in his early twenties, when the Pramukh brought him in the panchayat samiti. Two factors contributed to the rift that developed between them. First was, the Pramukh had promised Neta that he would give him contract works under the relief schemes which he failed to do. Secondly, the Pramukh had told Neta during the time of his election of MLA that he would resign and Neta would succeed him as Pramukh. He was elected MLA twice, first in 1969 and then in 1972, and on both occasions Neta worked for his success with "complete dedication and devotion." But whenever the notification for Pramukh's election came, and there was a talk of his successor, the Pramukh appeared to be procrastinating the matter. Actually what had happened meantime, the Pramukh had started realizing that Neta would not be under his control fully and started thinking of some other candidates as his successor.

On his part, Neta enhanced his academic qualifications by taking law degree. Some of the officials also coaxed him that he would not succeed in politics unless he got himself free from the Pramukh's control. They told him that he would never grow under Pramukh's 'shadow'. He was reminded, "Even the grass does not grow under a banian tree." Opponents of Pramukh in the panchayat samiti were looking forward for this opportunity. So they won over Neta Singh and decided for a vote of no confidence motion against the Pramukh. One of the intitiators of the move said, "When the rift developed between the Pramukh and Neta, I was happy. I wanted to demolish their bond so I encouraged Neta and spent both my time as well as money to bring a vote of no confidence. I wanted to be a spectator, and watch his castle under fire and enjoy it."

The vote of no confidence was a rare event, a strange spectacle. Three or four days before, kidnapping of the uncommitted and weak members had started from both the sides. These members were kept in safe places with tight security control. An ex-MLA was actively supporting Neta group. An influential rich man of the area, who had some previous enemity with the Pramukh rendered the services of his jeep to Neta. Jeeps lashed with *lathaits* were vying to catch hold of weak members so that they could be kidnapped.

Two members "ran away" from the block to avoid any kind of risk. On the eve of the meeting of the panchayat samiti, which was to discuss vote of no confidence, a beating-up incident took places, in which the Pramukh reportedly slapped a pro-Neta man. As a result, section 144 was enforced in the block.

In the meeting, the Pramukh's supporters sat in his chamber and did not attend the meeting. The Pramukh and a supporter of his attended the meeting but they did not put their signatures in the attendence register so they were not allowed to participate. Out of ten members who participated in the meeting, nine voted in favour of the resolution which expressed no confidence in the Pramukh. There was no vote against the resolution, president did not vote.

After the resolution, the Pramukh is alleged to have entered the PVP's chamber with a lieutenant of his, abused the PVP in the most offensive language and forcibly took away the proceedings register. The SDO and the thana incharge with all the police force, who were sitting there, were watching the scene as silent spectators.

The Pramukh objected about the resolution, on the ground that two third of the total members of the panchayat samiti should be present and participate in the voting. But the Up-Pramukh who presided over the meeting thought, since quorum was complete the resolution was valid. The statutory provision in this ragard is :

> "If the motion is carried with the support of not less than two third of the members of the panchayat samiti present and voting the Pramukh or the Up-Pramukh, as the case may be, shall cease to hold the office as such and shall be deemed to have vacated the same on and from the date on which the fact of the motion having been carried is affixed on the notice board of the office of panchayat samiti."

The Pramukh being a sitting Congress MLA maneouvered things in his favour in Patna. Within ten days, the DDC received a letter from the State Government asking him to withhold the

7. The Bihar Panchyat Samitis and Zila Parishads Act 1961, section 32 (2).

passed vote of no confidence motion against the Pramukh till government gave final orders. Till then, he would continue to remain the Pramukh. The government also asked him to supply all the relevant documents in that regard so that it could take a final decision.

Then, keeping all the material for more than a year and without giving sufficient opportunity to the opposite party for the representation, the resolution was cancelled. The cancelling letter was signed by an Under Secretary and was sent by a special messenger and read :

> "After necessary enquiry and scrutiny of the vote of no confidence resolution dated 23-10-73 against Mr ..., the Pramukh of ...panchayat samiti in Bhagalpur district, government has reached this decision, that the passed vote of no confidence resolution against that Pramukh, is unconstitutional. Therefore, using the powers vested in the Bihar panchayat samitis and zilla parishads act 1961, Section 78, government has invalidated that resolution."

The decision of the State government was not acceptable to the dissident faction and they filed a writ-petition in the high court on the ground that in invalidating a legally passed resolution government had exercised undue influence and malfidy. The appeal was in the court at the time of the study.

As a consequence of vote of no confidence incident, panchayat samiti was clearly divided into two antagonistic factions. Though it is reported, the Pramukh had virtually stopped coming to the block office after that incident, particularly till the first PVP was there, but he remained the leader of one of the two factions and Neta Singh emerged as the leader of the other faction. Since the factions have originated as a consequence of intra Rajput jealousy and rivalry, the leadership of both the factions is in the hands of Rajputs. As regards their followers, Neta faction has little more Rajputs and backwards, compared to the Pramukh's faction. Of the two brahmins, one is with the Pramukh and the other is with Neta faction. Similarly, in the Pramukh faction there are fewer active members compared to Neta faction. A good portion of the Pramukh supporters, particularly among the backward castes, are reported to be with him because they fear him and cannot stand against him.

An important development of the factionalism, particularly after the vote of no confidence incident, is the considerable decline in the influence of the Pramukh in the panchayat samiti. There were occasions when his resolutions were rejected by the majority vote. One such case was the censure of the first PVP which was dragged in four meetings of the samiti. But since the present PVP joined, his influence has increased mainly because the new PVP gives considerable importance to the Pramukh. Nevertheless, he cannot dictate the samiti to toe on his line any more after this incident. As a result, importance of individual members in the samiti has increased, particularly of the active ones.

An important aspect of the panchayat samiti politics is BDO's role vis-a-vis mukhiyas. During the first BDO's period, his actions were governed by the wishes of the Pramukh. Since three mukhiyas did not toe on line with the Pramukh so their panchayats were neglected. The second BDO stayed for a very short period, but during that period he did not discriminate the anti-Pramukh mukhiyas. During the period of the first PVP, it is reported by the Pramukh's supporters that their work was neglected by the PVP. He gave every possible help to the leader of the anti-Pramukh faction and gave more attention to their works. One of the Pramukh supporters said, "After the vote of no confidence, the work of those who supported the resolution was promptly attended and those who opposed it, neglected." As regards the present PVP, he claims that he is doing justice to all with no consideration for the factional alignments. The Pramukh faction would agree with the PVP. But some members of the anti-Pramukh faction felt that he was favouring the Pramukh faction. But one thing was clear, he was trying to win the confidence of the important members of both the factions.

As regards the subordinate staff's involvement in the samiti politics, through influential members, or receiving help from the Pramukh for furthering their interest, it has varied from time to time. During the period of the first BDO, the relations between him and the Pramukh were so good that there was hardly any scope for antagonising either the one or the other. The second BDO, though stayed for a short period, most of the office and some of the supervisory staff who were loyal to the Pramukh did not give the BDO full co-operation. The first PVP, when he joined faced the same problem. Therefore, the first thing he demanded was the transfer of all such staff and succeeded in transferring all except the veterinary doctor, whose transfer was stayed twice, thanks to the Pramukh's efforts. The new staff was loyal to the PVP and stood solidly behind him. The present PVP's duration has been very short and during this time there has not been any involvement of the staff in the samiti politics.

The Veterinary Doctor, a close confident of the Pramukh has been in the block for almost six years. He is said to have played the part of 'Manthara'[8] in intensifying the conflict between the Pramukh and the PVP. All the plans against the first PVP are reported to have been hatched at his residence. He rarely attends his office. Even for the present PVP he is an embarrassment. There is enough of ill-feeling in supervisory staff, the PVP seems to have compromised on this matter, knowing well that he is a close man of the Pramukh.

An important feature of the panchayat samiti politics is the emergence of new alignments, reshaping the factional politics. Author had the opportunity of witnessing a pre-election scene. The election of secretary of the 'vyapar mandal' an ex-officio members of the samiti was to take place, SDO court compound was the scene of intense political activity ten days before the election. One could notice small groups of mukhiyas discussing the question of a suitable choice. Neta had decided to support the sitting member. The Rajput ex-MLA, an arch enemy of the Pramukh for the last many years, who had played a very active role in the vote of no confidence also showed his interest in the election. Neta faction, this time, was far from united. Neta had promised his candidate a year earlier that he would again be the choice and wanted to stick to his words, whether the faction supported him or not, while others wanted a more cautious and calculated decision in this matter.

8. The analogy in drawn from the Ramayan, where Manthara, the maid of the queen Kaikai, coaxes the queen to ask King Dasharatha to give the kingdom to her son Bharat.

One member stated, "We don't want the group being divided on this issue. Because at present, Teja babu (the ex-MLA) is a choice of both the parties (he meant factions). The Pramukh when he comes back from Patna and knows that Neta is supporting the other candidate, will re-joice and support Teja babu." And that is what happened, when the Pramukh came, Teja babu was seen coming to the block office with him in his jeep. They sat together in the BDO's chamber. We are not in a position to comment about the consequences of this election[9] in reshaping the factional politics, but it must affect the balance of power in the samiti.

Like Raja ganj panchayat samiti, here also the CO plays an important role in the panchayat samiti politics. He is Bhumihar by caste and has good relations with the Pramukh. He has been in that place for over five years and was much closer to the Pramukh in comparison to the second BDO and the first PVP. During their times the Pramukh would visit his house but not theirs. The CO is very close to the Veterinary Doctor, who is his caste fellow. The Pramukh is obliged to the CO as he has some 'hats' and 'bazars' in his control which have not been vested to the government. The CO obliges the Pramukh by showing these in the official records in the Pramukh's private land. On his part the Pramukh obliges him by doing favours to him and his *jat bhai* the Veterinary Doctor.

9. The author had left Veerpur before the election took place. However, later reports indicated that Neta's candidate los 'and the Pramukh's won.

5

SUMMING UP

THE two panchayat samitis selected by us differed on three important points. Firstly, with regard to party control; in the one, the Pramukh was from the Congress (O), in the other, he was from the Congress (R).[1] Secondly; the one was a 'shadow package' block, the other was a 'non-shadow package' block. Thirdly ; the one was a block head-quarter only, the other was a sub-divisional headquarter also.

As regards Pramukh's party affiliation ; though in our case, we found the Congress (R) Pramukh was more powerful than the Congress (O) Pramukh. It was mainly because of the fact he has been a sitting Congress (R) MLA since 1969, having links with the influential politicians at the State level. In being an ex-zamindar of the area, at the local level also he had the traditional basis of authority. But generally speaking, Pramukh's party affilition was found to be inconsequential in matters of his power, prestige and dominance. We came accross cases where Pramukhs were quite influential and powerful despite the fact that they belonged to opposition parties. Pramukh's power and influence is dependent on four factors : (a) support from the member of the samiti ; (b) links with politicians and bureaucrats at the higher levels ; (c) holding public offices like MLA, MLC, chairman of a corporation, etc ; and (d) personal status in the area, and wealth.

Coming to the 'package' and the 'non-package' differences ; it was found that the PVPs, who were drawn from the Bihar Agricul-

1. Congress (R) was ruling party in the State, while Congress (O) was ruling party in the Zila Parishad at the time this study was conducted.

ture Service, were quite friendly and informal in their dealings with their subordinate staff. They were prone to adopt co-operation and extension techniques in the discharge of their duties. In contrast, the BDOs drawn from the Bihar Civil Service, were authoritative and formal in the dealings with their staff.

As regards the location of the block head quarter ; it was found that if the location of the block and the sub-divisional headquarter coincided, involvement of the outside elements in the samiti politics was greater in comparision to a situation where these two were separate. We found in case of Raja ganj, outside politics was subdued and it was confined to the block. In case of Veerpur, it would be more appropriate to quote the words of a staff, who had spent several years there ; "Politics is the life blood of Veerpur. You can feel it in the air the moment you enter here." Whether this is an exaggeration or not, but there is every reason to believe that a sub-divisional headquarter does provide a more fertile ground for the play of politics.

Coming to the question of conflicts between the officials and the non-officials, we find there are latent-manifest types of conflicts between them. The former type, we find among all the officials against all the non-officials and vice verse. This is a grudge which each 'set' has against the other. The officials think that the non-officials are useless, their co-operation is confined to big talks in the samiti meetings. They cause delay in the decision-making and unnecessarily interfere in the administrative sphere, where they should have no concern. They use resources of the samiti and their official position to preserve their own power positions and to further their personal ends. For the fulfilment of these ends they exercise unfair pressure on officials. The officials look upon them with contempt, as uneducated boors who create difficulties for the administration instead of solving them.

On the other side are non-officials, who have the image of their counterparts (ministers etc.), at the State level and think officials do not show due regard to them. They feel their role is neglected by the officials and they are not consulted in matters which are of public importance. They also resent the haughtiness and the superior air of the officials. Thus, both see each other as obstacles in the performance of their roles. This jeopardizes the basic principle of the panchayati raj. But the latent conflict does not lead to an open confrontation between the officials and the non-officials. This really creates ill-will between the two sets of functionaries and is caused by socio-economic and cultural differences between them, and the historical antecedents.

It is evident from our survey, that there is non-compatibility between the officials and the non-officials not only with regard to socio-economic traits but also marked differences in their attitudes and opinions, which sometimes are diametrically opposed. As regards socio-economic traits, officials are generally more educated, and younger in age, while the non-officials are generally less educated older in age but richer compared to the officials. In the sphere of attitudes and opinions also, both the sets generally, talk negatively about each other.

The second type of conflict is manifest and is caused by specific incidents or cases, pertaining to a set of items e.g., use of block jeep, transfer of samiti employees, power prerogatives, etc. This type of conflict generally does not polarize into a conflict of officials versus non-officials. By and large it is caused by the BDO and the Pramukh not seeing eye to eye. These two, who head the two teams at the panchayat samiti level are the chief actors of panchayat samiti politics. Their good or bad relations symbolise, good or bad relations between the officials and the non-officials.

As regards the question of relations between the Pramukh and the BDO, it must be kept in mind that cordial relations between the two per se, is neither a necessary nor a sufficient condition for the success of the panchayati raj. We find, sometimes relations are extremely good between them but they do not work in the interest of the community. Instead, they become active collaborators in misusing samiti resources and facilities for furthering their personal ends. This is a worse situation in comparison to the one where there is a tension and conflict but one of them is not allowing the other to misuse his office and powers. An ideal situation would be one, where cordial relations obtain between the two and both think in terms of the larger interest of the community rather than narrow interests of a segment or their own personal interests.

The Pramukh has two things in his mind. First, he is a Pramukh because he is a mukhiya, so he tries to get maximum benefits of the block agency to his panchayat so that he could get re-elected mukhiya next time. Secondly, he is a Pramukh because of the support of the majority of the members of the samiti, so he tries to satisfy them. In case the BDO is willing to satisfy the Pramukh in these two respects there are good relations between them. But if the BDO does not want to oblige him in these respects there are tensions and conflicts. In addition, Pramukhs are generally interested in using their office for their personal benefits and if the BDO is an accommodating type, they collaborate and go hand in hand, otherwise a powerful Pramukh creates all sorts of difficulties for the BDO.

There is hardly any conflict in the matter of policy implementation. Conflicts is seldom caused because of the vagueness or ambiguity of the statutory provisions and the rules and the regulations. Generally, tensions arise on account of routine administrative matters, power prerogatives, clash of personalities and vested interests. The most common items of conflicts are: (a) Distribution of government facilities through the agency of block e.g., agricultural loans, subsidy for the construction of wells, etc.; (b) Command over panchayat samiti resources ; (c) Control over the block jeep ; (d) Administrative control over samiti personnel ; and (e) transfer of the subordinate staff within the block.

As regards the question of dual authority, there is not much place for it in the theory. The non-officials are expected to take policy-decisions and implementation is the responsibility of the officials under the over all supervision of the BDO. But partly because of the vagueness in the statutory provision[2] and partly because of the pattern of relationship existing between the ministers and the civil servants at the State level, which Pramukhs' have in their minds, they interfere in routine administrative

2. The Bihar Panchayat Samitis and Zila Parishads Act, 1961, says : "The Pramukh shall exercise administrative control over the Block Development Officer for the implementation of the decisions and resolutions of the Panchayat samiti and the standing committees therof" [Section 19 (d)].

matters. It creates difficulty for the subordinate staff when relations between the Pramukh and the BDO are bad. In such a situation they sometimes receive contradictory orders from the Pramukh and the BDO and it is a difficult choice for them to obey the one or the other without displeasing one of them. It affects their efficiency and morale, no doubt, but it creates another difficulty for the BDO concerning obedience and discipline. For instance, granting of casual leave to a peon is BDO's job, but if the Pramukh starts granting it, or, if the BDO punishes a VLW and the Pramukh condones it ; they would not give any importance to the BDO's instructions.

Coming to the question of collaboration and cooperation between officials and non-officials, we find, if both officials as well as non-officials have their own axe to grind they become active collaborators and do not hesitate in misusing public funds and governmental facilities for their personal gains. On the contrary, if they think from the viewpoint of public work, they can utilize their offices for this purpose and can be effective instruments of community development. The Pramukh being a public representative can directly write to the higher authorities, both official and political, and draw their attention to the local problems. We found, where they used their offices for the public work, Pramukhs were successful. Politics then becomes functional for the community, both useful as well as necessary. But collaboration takes an extreme form if a corrupt Pramukh has a samiti's overwhelming support and a willing BDO to help him in his personal gains. Under such circumstances they become active collaborators, misusing the samiti resources and facilities for their personal gains.

In the context of the relationship between the BDO and the other staff, it was found that if the relations between the Pramukh and the BDO were good there were no problems except in a few cases. In case their relations were strained the officials often aligned themselves with the Pramukh.

In some cases it was found that the relations between the BDO and MO or Veterinary Doctor were not good. The main reason being, in professional education doctors do not consider themselves in any way inferior to the BDO and most often their salary was more than BDO's. They feel the BDO, as the captain of the team should seek co-operation from them rather than boss over them.

The problem which is generally faced by the 'subject matter specialists' is that of dual administrative control over them. They receive orders from both their departmental officers and the BDO. They feel, it is very difficult to satisfy the both.

Among the staff, there are three conspicuous divisions ; the first consists of the field staff mainly the VLWs and Panchayat Sewaks, the second consists of the supervisory staff, the third consists of the office staff. Status wise, the clerical staff is not higher than the field staff, but they appeared to be most powerful owing to their control over the official records and the papers. In government organizations, especially in developing countries, there exists the phenomenon of 'file syndrome', in which every thing has to go according to set rules and procedures. It is mainly due to this that 'staff'[3], though it has a secondary role to aid and advice becomes all powerful. The field staff generally resent the behaviour of the office staff, particularly towards their clients (villagers). The field staff bring them to the block for getting their work done, but they are made to run many times by the office staff, before their work is done, and that too not until the office staff is gratified.

Generally the BDOs, who are interested in self gratification depend on some 'trusted' member of the staff for this purpose. Because of the BDO's dependence on him, this gentleman exercises great influence over the BDO. Irrespective of his official status, he is defacto second only to the BDO in terms of power. This causes a general resentment and dissatisfaction among rest of the officials, and demoralises them if this 'link man' of the BDO happens to hold lower position in the official set up of the block.

3. The concept of 'line' and 'staff', developed first in military organization, was borrowed from there and applied to civil organization and administration. 'Line' refers to functionaries who are concerned with the direct achievement of the main purpose of the organization. while, 'staff' refers to those who assist 'line' in their work.

The relations between the Pramukh and other members of the panchayat samiti are determined by several factors. The most important of these is the factional politics. The factional politics subsumes all other factors. The most common factor in the formation of factions is caste. Another factor which is important for attracting a member to a particular faction is the benefits he can derive from the Pramukh, for himself as well as for his panchayat. The factions are generally formed because of inter-caste feeling. However, sometimes intra-caste rivalry and jealousy also cause the formation of a faction.

We find that the support or opposition to the Pramukh is on neither party nor ideological lines. The Pramukh generally gets support from the members of his faction irrespective of the merit of his case and is opposed on all such matters by the opposition faction. The Pramukh invariably helps his own faction members more with regard to the services and facilities given through the agency of the block. A common complaint by the members of the opposition faction is that they are neither given enough facilities nor adequate funds, and development work in their panchayats is neglected. This problem is more acute in case opposition faction is very small and the BDO is a yes-man of the Pramukh.

Who dominates the show ? The Pramukh or the BDO ? The deciding factor is the extent of the support the Pramukh gets from the samiti. If the Pramukh has a solid majority behind him he is bound to dominate over the BDO. Under such circumstances the BDO shrinks into a passive instrument, an inert pawn in the manipulative hands of the Pramukh. The BDO being a careerist, who comes to work in a particular block for a short duration, and would not want to get involved in unnecessary tussles with the Pramukh to spoil his chances of promotion. On the other hand, if the Pramukh has a thin majority and some of his supporters are oscilating type, the BDO is in an advantageous position. In such a case the BDO dominates because he can always manoeuver some of the members of the samiti to disturb the thin majority of the Pramukh. Here the Pramukh is in a constant danger of losing his office so he plays second fiddle to the BDO.

Another factor which is important in the case of Pramukh is, whether he holds some important public office, like the membership of State assembly or the Council, the chairmanship of some public corporation etc., or not ? In case he holds and has links with the higher level officials and the politicians, he can manage things in his favour even if he has lost ground at the local level.

It is discouraging to note that there are no institutional or in-built arrangements having the potential to solve the tensions and conflicts that have existed from the beginning. The most common informal machanism, in case of a deadlock between the Pramukh and the BDO, is the reconciliation effort made by the influential or neutral members of the samiti to bring them together over a feast or a tea party. Sometimes, higher authorities like the DDC or the ADC also approach the warring parties for a reproachment.

Greater participation of the sub-divisional and district level officers in the meetings of the panchayat samiti can be helpful in bringing about greater co-operation and co-ordination among them, and between the officials and non-officials. Unfortunately resolution after resolution are passed by the panchayat samiti showing a resentment of the samiti over the regular absenteeism on the part of officials. Thus, we find this institutional arrangement for achieving better co-ordination and co-operation has not been utilized.

We had started with the presumption that harmonious relations between the officials and the non-officials is a *sine qua non* for the success of the panchayati raj. Our findings, however, in the light of this presumption show that it is neither a necessary nor a sufficient condition for the community development purposes. Panchayati raj is not an end in itself, it is rather a democratic means to achieve socio-economic transformation of our rural societies. Therefore, it is not sufficient that these two 'sets' work harmoniously. It is more important that they should work for the public good. The achilles' heel of the panchayati raj system is that it encourages 'politics' for personal gains, where it is unnecessary and harmful, and denies 'politics' where it is necessary and useful for the community welfare purposes.

It would not be out of context to mention that the structural reforms are not the panacea of the ills of the panchayati raj. The more important thing is the ultimate purpose we are looking for. If the conflict between the two sets, officials and non-officials, is the fundamental problem, it is not difficult to eliminate it by placing the officials under the non-officials, in the similar fashion as secretaries work under the ministers in the States and the Centre. The important question is, whether it will solve the problems or will it create other problems of greater dimensions ?

It is not very relevant to talk in terms of solutions or reform proposals. The major shortcomings of the panchayati raj system are inherent in the larger socio-political culture, or are part of the historical antecedents. Under such circumstances any reforms at the grass roots will bear the stamp of ritualism, which will not change the system fundamentally. For instance, whether an MLA should be allowed to be a Pramukh or not ? This question does not have any definite yes or no answer. It has both the sides ; if the Pramukh is committed to the welfare of his community, he can utilize his position as an MLA for its welfare. On the other hand, if he uses his office for his personal advantage then his constituency people will suffer. Therefore, what is needed is an enlightened and committed leadership, and efficient and development minded officers. This raises the question ; can we get such leaders and officers ? The answer will be conditional : yes, if the larger socio-political culture is congenial to their growth.

INDEX